THE VAXXED

Culture War in the Workplace

Shawn A. McCastle, MBA, MSIOP

THE VAXXED

CULTURE WAR IN THE WORKPLACE

Shawn A. McCastle, MBA, MSIOP

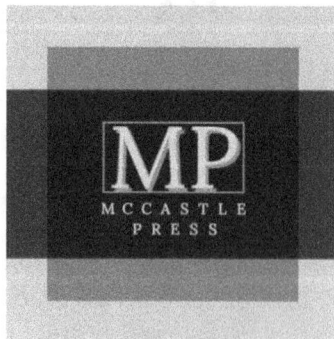

www.mccastlepress.com

Copyright

Published by McCastle Press, Conyers, Georgia

(in a limited association with Primedia eLaunch LLC for eBook only.)

Publisher's Website: www.mccastlepress.com

Author's Website: www.shawnmccastle.com

Twitter: @shawnmccastle

ISBN: 979-8-9856957-1-7 (hardcover)

ISBN: 979-8-9856957-0-0 (paperback)

ISBN: 978-1-64826-787-1 (e-book)

First Edition: January 2022

Library of Congress Cataloging-in-Publication Data

Name: McCastle, Shawn Anthony, 1978-author

Title: The Vaxxed: culture war in the workplace / Shawn Anthony McCastle

Description: First Edition. | Conyers, GA

Identifiers: LCCN 2021923420 | ISBN: 979-8-9856957-1-7 (hardcover) | ISBN: 979-8-9856957-0-0 (paperback) | ISBN: 978-1-64826-787-1 (e-book)

Subjects: | Job Satisfaction. | Work—psychological aspects. | Labor.

This book includes biographical references.

Cover design: McCastle Press

Printed in the United States of America.

Legal Notice

Contents

Contents

Contents

Contents

Contents

Contents

Contents

Preface

This book is about people, not just any people the terminated, unvaccinated employees. It is about me, you, and everyone else who goes to work daily, expecting a social net to catch your back in times of adversity. The toughest time employees have had to live through is coronavirus (i.e., COVID-19), especially after the lockdowns had begun.

Most people had never witnessed or experienced the brutality a pandemic and a lockdown can hold over one's psyche, the rigid muscles, the difficulty sleeping, the inability to concentrate, and the addle thoughts, to name a few.

This book is about the horrors of the unvaccinated, the social isolation, the loss of relationships, the lack of means to provide for oneself, all, simply because an employee made an unpopular choice about his or her bodily integrity, which others have disagreed with. ***As a terminated, unvaccinated employee, it is like being on the fifth-grade playground all over again, you are the strangest child the other children have ever seen, simply because you are different. "Oh, he got the cooties!" You know, the fanciful disease from childhood for the socially undesirable****. And all you know is, **everyone is looking at you like you have two left shoes on***.

The United States is supposed to be the land of the free, but the terminated, unvaccinated employees have found themselves being burned at the stake by corporate policies and procedures and intolerant people often misguided by what is presented in the daily news and on social media.

I had worked at the World Bank Group headquarters in Washington D.C. for Allied-Universal Security Services since 2018 as a building supervisor and was a sworn, Special Police Sergeant until September 21, 2021.

In their wisdom, (even after being forced to work through the COVID-19 pandemic) I was terminated with all the other unvaccinated employees who did not get vaccinated by September 7, 2021 (which later changed to September 20, 2021).

Though the termination was unjust, it is cathartic to be free from microaggression, micromanagement, misleading information, overinflated egos, and gaslighting. I can sleep well at night now. My termination caused a deep reflection on my experience working for organizations that lack basic ethics. I have never worked for organizations that will assign their employees to perform a task and then turn around and fire them for performing the same task.

Working at the World Bank Group was one of the most humiliating work experiences I have had in my entire work history, and I was a supervisor. I have tried to explain this to my friends, and they even lacked the understanding of what I explained to them, even though I have articulated my thoughts well. My friends did not believe it. When an organization has governmental immunity, it is a different type of work environment.

I had driven back to Washington D.C., arriving back from a two-week vacation after being at home in Rockdale County, Georgia. At about 05:14 hours on September 21, 2021, Captain William Bullock, my supervisor, informed me that I would not be able to work. As I peered over at Bullock, with his unamused look, I asked why. I could hear my own voice crack with alarm. As I asked Bullock to call Rick Lewis, my manager, my thoughts marched in my mind.

With knees knocking and heavy hands, I waited like an errant child as Bullock called twice, with no answer. Then, a few moments later, Rick called back. After some brief back and forth between Bullock and Rick, Bullock asked me: "Are you vaccinated?" As I drafted this book, I heard those words ringing: Are you vaccinated? I knew right then; the sledgehammer had dropped. I was being displaced from the workplace. At that point, the apprehension had eaten into me. Dismayed by the events of the moment. I still pressed through, indeed. Indeed, I kept pushing.

As I walked from deep within the well of the World Bank Group's main campus for the last time, I savored the moment. I knew I would never scan my credentials on the turnstiles again. I knew Bill Johnson (Project Manager) and Rick would be eager to distribute a "be on the lookout" (BOLO), immediately: deactivating my credentials and plastering my photo for all my former colleagues to observe. I knew I would never be greeted by security professionals Cummings and Hartwell again. And finally, I knew many work relationships that I held would wane over the next few months. I tasted the bitter pill, the cruel hypocrisy.

Security professionals and Special Police Officers working at the World Bank Group were required to work through the pandemic; so, I did not and still do not understand the rationale for my termination. I was the voice of reason, the conscious. In the background, I was telling the leadership: "It is a better way to do business than by mass terminations."

While working at the World Bank Group, I experienced some crazy things, to say the least, but COVID-19 topped them all. This book is written not to embarrass neither the World Bank Group nor Allied-Universal Security Services, but to share my lived experience. There are a lot of socially uncouth and private things I could reveal about each organization, but that is not going to resolve the COVID-19 pandemic or make the terminated, unvaccinated employees whole again, so I will reserve my thoughts.

During my employment at the World Bank Group, I had observed about 22 security officers or Special Police Officers arrive to work contaminated with COVID-19. Generally, Special Police Officers would arrive to work sick, because the sick and safe policies were inconsistently administered. As an example, I even received corrective action through the unevenly dispensed sick and safe policies and practices. After three years free of no call-offs or tardiness, I received a chronic absenteeism corrective action after taking three non-consecutive sick days in a city that requires employers to compensate its employees for seven paid sick days (with the associated time off). I know, when I received my corrective action, I was thinking the same thing, "what the hell?" Believe me, I was pissed. "I thought, what the hell is wrong with these people?"

The District of Columbia Department of Health may not have gathered data on those 22 security officers or Special Police Officers because they often traveled from Maryland and Virginia to work at the World Bank Group.

I took measures (beyond stated guidelines) to ensure that I would not be exposed to COVID-19 while working. I followed social distancing. I attended to hygiene factors such as washing my hands frequently. I engaged in the least physical contact possible. Oh, and of course, I wore a mask. As a supervisor, I even directed employees to be tested for COVID-19 or go to the hospital after noticing they had COVID-19-like symptoms.

In December 2019, like most people, we began hearing about coronavirus (COVID-19), as news stories began to emerge. As early as February 2020, there were rumors of closures, but those closures did not occur until March 2020. Being naturally inquisitive, and as a social science researcher, I began looking through the scientific data that can only be accessed through databases such as ProQuest and medical databases.

I recall reading that up to a million people could die in the United States from COVID-19 alone. This was when there was public debate about who had produced the best COVID-19 model. I instantly thought this is going to be a wild ride, a big deal for the people I work with and for the world.

My motivation for authoring this book involves what I see as an encroachment of our civil liberties, not directly through the United States government, but through semi-government actors (i.e., employers) to which the government can hold plausible deniability.

A subtler motivation is what I see as a house divided, falling apart. The COVID-19 pandemic has divided people in unimaginable ways, ways that would have never been thought of before. And as I thought about it increasingly, I thought to myself, "we need a President George W. Bush moment," while standing at ground zero he said: "I can hear you!" However, no one is listening to the hurting. To the broken-hearted. To the vulnerable.

My inspiration for this book began when I decided to write a LinkedIn article. So, this is my LinkedIn article, the long format. I thought about the information in this book since my termination, but never took any concrete steps to start on it. But one day, I happened to be in a deep discussion with one of my closest confidants, and I decided to draft an article, but after I began researching the topic, I could not simply settle for an article. And when I began, I could not stop writing.

I took a scholarly approach while researching and drafting this book.

I wanted to share some things about myself. But what has prevented me from writing books in the past is that I am introverted and incredibly private. I had to first overcome self-imposed obstacles. And then, I had to tackle the overwhelming data that keeps coming about unvaccinated employees and COVID-19.

This book has a little of me, a little research, and a little about others' experiences.

Since I had been working on my dissertation at LIGS University (Ph.D. in Management), completed Ph.D. (Business Administration) coursework at Trident University International, finished a Master of Business Administration at the University of the People, completed a Master of Science in Industrial-Organizational Psychology at the University of Phoenix at the School of Advanced Studies, earned dual Bachelor of Arts in Organizational Management and Psychology (both summa cum laude) from the University of Arizona Global Campus, and received an Associate of General Studies from the Northwestern State University of Louisiana, I had been writing for a while, so I was familiar with certain layouts and formats and some book requirements. So, naturally, I had some basic understanding of authoring a book. A dissertation is a book, scholarly and well researched.

One of the things that I struggled with in drafting this book is disclosure. But the circumstances of the moment challenged me. The situation prodded me. And I answered the call, and I found myself writing about the unsexy nature of a job that was not supposed to be political.

My job was superseded by politics. Though I worked at an international organization, my job had not been about politics before COVID-19. But somehow, after March 2020 when COVID-19 became a pandemic, my work as a Special Police Sergeant and supervisor became a political punching bag. Unfortunately, when an issue has political undertones, what generally gets lost in the discussion is the people. And I was one of the persons lost in the translation, the unvaccinated, terminated employees.

I have had the opportunity to work with some fine and professional people and some not-so-professional people. I had the opportunity to be in the same space as kings, presidents, and prime ministers—world leaders—you name it.

When the World Bank Group policymakers were implementing their policies to terminate people for COVID-19, I was there in the same rooms, I received the same emails, and I saw the discrimination and fall out from those decisions, but I kept my mouth closed and did my job, what I was paid to do, which was to ensure their physical safety. And I did protect their physical safety without fear and reservation.

One of the last things I did was notice and contact a male subject, who when contacted, admitted to being at the World Bank Group for three days, (unannounced) arriving from California and waiting for the VP of HR. Yet in still, I was discarded and terminated.

This book is for the many people who were disregarded and trashed for simply something your constitutional rights allow you to do, make basic decisions about your bodily integrity.

After the release of this book, some may argue, one way or another, and some may suggest that I am in the antivaccination camp, which represents the furthermost untruth, I am in the pro-constitution camp. As a scientist myself, I want science to win.

Yours truly,

Shawn A. McCastle, MBA, MSIOP
Wednesday, January 26, 2022 – Conyers, Georgia

Dedication

I dedicate this book to my mother, the late Geraldine Houston Buckley (sunset 2017), and my father, the late Douglas McCastle, Sr. (sunset 2010). My mom was the mom my God handpicked for me. My father was an old-school, hard worker. He worked until his hard-worked and worn body would not allow him to work any further. Every time I think about how hard my father worked, it motivates me to make the workplace better for others.

Acknowledgment

A book, especially one that addresses work, and the workplace must be well thought out, which leads me to acknowledge a few people.

I am graciously indebted to a few people whom I would like to acknowledge on my first book journey.

First, I would like to thank Ralph B. Lee, Jr. and Wendy Lee. They are some of the coolest people I know. Ralph has been a sounding board, listening to all my off-the-wall ideas. You are much appreciated. Thank you.

Second, I would like to thank Jeff R. Hayes. Jeff is a loyal friend, one who helped me see things from different perspectives with his keen insights and depth of wisdom. Thank you for sharing in such a long and lasting friendship.

Third and finally, I would like to thank Chanell Michelle McCastle, my wife and loyal friend. I have spent many nights reading, researching, writing, and working. Through it all, you have been there for me. Thank you.

Epigraph

The hardworking farmer must be first to partake of the crops.

—2 Timothy 2:6, New King James Version

We need to do a better job of putting ourselves higher on our own 'to do' list.

—Michelle Obama

Greed is not a financial issue. It's a heart issue.

—Andy Stanley

Without equity, we cannot end COVID-19, HIV or any other pandemic.

—Peter Sands

This pandemic has magnified every existing inequality in our society – like systemic racism, gender inequality, and poverty.

—Melinda Gates

Introduction

Dignity not only explains an aspect of what it means to be human, but is a hallmark of our shared humanity. Everyone wants to be treated in a way that shows they matter. —Donna Hicks

I recall sitting in my office at the International Finance Corporation (IFC), about a 13 or 14-minute walk to the White House, on January 6, 2021, the evening shift. I received a call from one of my closest friends. I could hear a strange concern in his voice. As I listened, all I could imagine was, this cannot be true. What could not be true? My friend said to me: "Some guy is sitting in the president's seat with a Viking-style hat on." The person who we now know as Jacob Chansley, whom news outlets dubbed the "QAnon shaman," was sitting in the seat of the president of the Senate.

When I turned on the news, it was all over the news and social media. I was mortified. Here I am sitting about 2.5 miles down the street from this attempted coup of the United States government and did not know what was going on.

Most Americans are clueless about what is truly going on with their government, just like I was clueless about the January 6, 2021, incident at the United States Capitol. The same can be said for employees working for corporations, they simply fail to comprehend the inner workings of the workplace, for example, why are they working all those hours for the same wage they were working for three, five, or nine years ago.

The seriousness and weight of this book reach into the workplace, social issues, and discuss COVID-19. A pervasive realism exists, and it is compounded by inherent socioeconomic disadvantages and social power dynamics. Power differentials exist today and have existed historically (L. Smith, 2010). And such power dynamics are not going anywhere.

This book discusses the gritty, posterior issues of COVID-19 and the mass terminations that rock the United States. Comparisons of the COVID-19 pandemic and the AIDS epidemic are made, showing how society is no better off today than yesterday by terminating the employment of employees who refused to provide their vaccination status or submit to COVID-19 vaccination at all.

I share first-hand experiences and thoughts about ethically dealing with employees. In addition, the book discusses real problems that must be addressed regarding employment in the aftermath, post-COVID-19.

I was working as a sworn, Special Police Sergeant and supervisor at the World Bank Group for Allied-Universal Security Services while I was completing my Ph.D. in Management. I worked when scheduled and to minimize friction with my employer, I arrived on time all the time.

I had worked for Allied-Universal Security Services in Georgia, and I resigned from the company because they seemed to have payroll problems weekly. I would work 40 hours and my check would be 20 hours. Although my supervisor Joe would have the problem fixed, this payroll problem persisted for six months before I had enough. When one works for low wages, this could be the difference between the lights getting turned off and eating. And this problem was a consistent weekly problem, so I left the company.

I was employed with American Security Programs (ASP) in September 2018, and in March 2021, ASP announced that Allied-Universal Security Services had bought them out. Imagine how disappointed and dismayed I was when that announcement was made that Allied-Universal Security Services was taking over. So, this is how I ended up being reemployed with Allied-Universal Security Services.

American Security Programs, a SecurAmerica company, had won the contract with the World Bank Group in 2018. American Security Programs' first official day taking over the contract from Allied-Universal Security Services was October 1, 2018. The transition was unorganized. Special Police Officers and security officers did not have the proper uniforms and equipment.

Not only did Allied-Universal Security Services acquire ASP, but the company also acquired G4S Security Solutions. So, Allied-Universal Security Services has become a behemoth of a company, and such acquisitions represent a mission of security domination. G4S Security Solutions had held the title of the largest security service provider before the Allied Barton Security Services and Universal Services of America merger.

Business mergers commonly occur without Sherman Act or Clayton Act violations. Allied-Universal Security Services is the largest security company in the world. Like the heavily regulated banking and telecommunications industries, Allied-Universal Security Services has merged its way into becoming the security industry. When one thinks about a corporation of this size, it becomes reminiscent of 2008: "Too big to fail."

An example of the too big to fail status is noted by Sachs (2020) who reported that the City of Denver, Colorado nixed a contract with Allied-Universal Security Services which already holds a large footprint in Denver, Colorado. After the acquisition of G4S Security Solutions and ASP, a SecurAmerica company, the City of Denver's selection of security operations was extensively reduced, which means Allied-Universal Security Services wins contracts by extension, or if not, they just acquisition the company from whoever holds the contract. Recall, ASP won the contract from the World Bank Group and Allied-Universal Security Services acquired ASP roughly two and a half years later. It seems a little hinky.

By working at the World Bank Group, I have witnessed how the marriage between Allied-Universal Security Services and the World Bank Group functions. None of their practices directly impacted me, initially. But then, an earlier incident in 2018 left me a little alarmed, because I thought that I might have to arrest one of the World Bank Group's managers for an assault on a female manager that I witnessed. The assault incident provided a small window into the world to which I found myself.

When companies contract with the World Bank Group, they essentially give their soul to the World Bank Group, because in my view, it seemed whatever the World Bank Group asked, these companies' managers would get down on their knees looking forward at the bank.

The contract creep became so egregious that I penned an email to management. In my email dated Friday, July 30, 2021, I said: "Sometimes, I believe that I may show up to work and be assigned to clean toilets in my Special Police Officer uniform and gun belt because of the lack of boundaries and constraints of such partnership [between the World Bank Group and Allied-Universal Security Services], especially a complete disregard for all stakeholders' feedback." I provide law enforcement, not maintenance.

So, in this book, I share my COVID-19 pandemic experience, including my termination from the World Bank Group and Allied-Universal Security Services.

As I sat here waiting for an answer from Allied-Universal Security Services about my religious accommodation, one month passed. Then, the next month passed. And all I could do was twiddle my thumbs from the ambiguous loss.

I knew the accommodation process did not work that way. In fact, in a dissenting opinion, Justice Gorsuch of the United States Supreme Court wrote in the case *John Does 1–3, et al. v. Janet T. Mills, Governor of Maine, et al. 595 U. S. _____ (2021)* said:

> The First Amendment protects the exercise of sincerely held religious beliefs... Laws that single out sincerely held religious beliefs or conduct based on them for sanction are 'doubtless . . . unconstitutional...' A State may not assume 'the best' of individuals engaged in their secular lives while assuming 'the worst' about the habits of religious persons.... Slice it how you will, medical exemptions and religious exemptions are on comparable footing when it comes to the State's asserted interests... If human nature and history teach anything, it is that civil liberties face grave risks when governments proclaim indefinite states of emergency... Many other States have made do with a religious exemption in comparable vaccine mandates... [The] decision to deny a religious exemption in these circumstances doesn't just fail the least restrictive means test, it borders on the irrational. (pp. 1-8)

Again, as the United States Supreme Court has asserted in *United States v. Peters, 9 U.S. 115* (1809) and reasserted by Justice Roberts on December 10, 2021, in Whole Woman's Health, et al. v. Austin Reeve Jackson, Judge, District Court of Texas, 114th District, et al. 595 U. S. _____ (2021) that "if the legislatures of the several states may, at will, annul the judgments of the courts of the United States, and destroy the rights acquired under those judgments, the constitution itself becomes a solemn mockery" ("Opinion of Roberts, C. J.," p. 4).

Justices Gorsuch and Roberts' opinions expressly deal with government issues, so I know that private industry surely cannot violate my rights the way I was violated at the World Bank Group and with Allied-Universal Security Services.

Understanding the Book's Structure
This book is divided into three parts with 34 chapters.

Chapter One through Five

Chapters one through five delves into what drove the mass terminations in the United States. Chapter one specifically notes that there were stark differences in how European employers addressed the COVID-19 pandemic than how the United States employers handled employees during the COVID-19 pandemic.

Chapters Six and Seven

Chapters six and seven address emotional safety, psychological safety, and organizational controls.

Chapter Eight

Chapter eight specifically looks at what employers have done to employees after COVID-19 through mass terminations.

Chapter Nine

Chapter nine looks at a historical example of what has happened to others through the lens of history to show the damage past events have pushed on society.

Chapters Ten and Eleven

Chapters 10 and 11 show how society is no better off using large-scale mass termination. The chapters show that national and international progress is damaged through mass termination and show the unforced errors of the COVID-19 pandemic.

Chapter 12

Chapter 12 sums up the effect of what will happen when politicians realize such large-scale damage has occurred to the workforce through unforced errors, especially when they understand the second-order effects of a mass termination.

Chapter 13

Chapter 13 addresses the prestidigitation and reasoning behind many of the return-to-work policies.

Chapter 14 and 15

Chapters 14 and 15 look at the greedy institutions, greedy work, narcissistic organizations, and the consequences of working for these types of organizations in the COVID-19 pandemic.

Chapter 16

Chapter 16 addresses the rulers (i.e., organizations) and the ruled (i.e., the employees). Understanding how the gears of the corporate world work give others a sense of why the environment has become toxic.

Chapter 17

Chapter 17 addresses the return-to-work policies in more detail. Returning to work has been more burdensome because employers failed to consider why most employees were working remotely in the first place.

Chapter 18 and 19

Chapters 18 and 19 investigated how people are suffering and issues of conformity and shame.

Chapter 20

Chapter 20 investigated the personal experience of the author and what occurred at his employer, Allied-Universal Security Services at the World Bank Group.

Chapter 21

Chapter 21 looks at two issues: rankism and caste as a system in the workplace.

Chapter 22

Chapter 22 looks at the Biden administration's COVID-19 plan, briefly.

Chapter 23

Chapter 23 investigates employee autonomy and why it is important to any return-to-work efforts.

Chapter 24 through 33

Chapter 24 through 33 look into the AIDS epidemic and the COVID-19 pandemic and makes comparisons.

The Final Word

Chapter 34 ties up the information of this book by drawing on all the information to conclude The Vaxxed: Culture War in the Workplace.

Part 1

Chapter 1

A Breath of Honesty

*It seems our collective capacity to consider —
simultaneously — the many sides to a decision is
weak, if not nonexistent. We crave certainty in
some (any!) aspect of our lives, and the
pressures of the moment reinforce our natural
tendency toward confirmation bias. —Morela
Hernandez*

Organizations recognize the pluralism and counterparty risk between their corporations and their employees, even when applicants and employees fail to do so. Even then, something vastly unethical is afoot in the workplace, and with it, employees can observe their true value and worth. So, let us begin by being honest.

Being honest means, employees have martyred themselves to the workplace at the behest of corporate policies.

Being honest means, employees have sacrificed their utility in the name of someone else's corporate wealth for years.

Being honest means, organizations must admit that they are the center of employees bartering their utility for trinkets.

Being honest means, employees have put aside some of life's most valuable time to be with their families and friends to go to work.

Being honest means, employees have worked in a system without proper medical care, nutritional care, and psychological care.

Being honest means, employees have been dumped, diminished, and denied, while at the same time being dazzled and dazed by carrots and sticks, with more daze than dazzle.

Moreover, since we are being honest, everyone knows the workplace will never be the same. Never! According to Pisani (2021), it is a fallacy to believe a vaccine will restore organizations to pre-pandemic settings and globalization patterns. Ashton (2021) noted that "things aren't going back to normal because this is our new normal" (p. 3). And for the new normal, Wetrich (2021) called for a wholesale organizational change, the complete retooling of how organizations function.

The COVID-19 pandemic has altered organizations' operations now and far into the future (Rudolph & Zacher, 2021). Before the pandemic, Elkington et al. (2008) noted that the world was already experiencing inescapable change that involves culture, economics, and most importantly how people view themselves, what they believe, and what they will tolerate.

The COVID-19 pandemic only accelerated the changes whether for good or bad, these changes are coming.

Not only have organizations been changed, but also Gingrich (2020) noted that a slew of changes will be everlasting for the future of the United States, including how Americans experience and make sense of the United States going forward. Thus, nation-states, corporations, and people will be forever changed, post-pandemic (Zakaria, 2020).

The alarm bells are ringing everywhere. What alarm bells? The bells announcing that Democracy within the United States is in jeopardy of failing. The bells are ringing so loud that Edsall (2021) noted a large number of published articles and discussions have increased on the subject of Democracy failing. Attorney and law professor Richard L. Hasen (as cited in Gellman, 2021) observed that "the democratic emergency is already here" (para. 4). More importantly, when adverse events occur, according to Taleb (2010), "negative ones [i.e., Black Swans] happen very quickly" ("A Black Swan is Relative to Knowledge," para. 2).

Pildes (2021) noted that political fragmentation, which has led to multiple tribes with power, makes it difficult for democratic governments to operate well. While political fragmentation may well rest at the center of many issues, this still does not properly account for how the leadership of the United States allows management by crisis approach to effectuate policy. While the management by crisis strategy moves the needle for a while, such tactics always require more effort, more intervention, and more government. It requires so much government that people cannot seem to get government out of their lives in one form or another.

For example, in the run-up to the war on terror (2003), the United States government had urged citizens to get duct tape and plastic sheets to seal their windows in case of a terrorist attack (Meserve, 2003). The 1950s are famous for useless duck-and-cover drills (protection for the

Atom bomb dropping) that probably caused more psychological trauma than the drills were worth (Pruitt, 2019). In the financial crisis of 2007–2008, the United States government used what it had learned in the 50s, fear works. And unfortunately, today, every time something significant occurs, the United States government has begun to use fear against its own people.

Eventually, the people who purchased duct tape and plastic sheets, the ones who jumped under tables, and the ones who capitulated to give the bankers billions of taxpayer money will become weary and worn out. The weariness has already shown its ugly face on January 6, 2021, which is just a sign of a larger problem festering underneath an ill that has overtaken the voices of reason, spiritual blackout.

We do not have to wait to see the social, political, and psychological results of spiritual blackout. According to the International Institute of Democracy and Electoral Assistance (2021):

The world is becoming more authoritarian as autocratic regimes become even more brazen in their repression. Many democratic governments are backsliding and are adopting authoritarian tactics by restricting free speech and weakening the rule of law, a trend exacerbated by the Covid-19 pandemic. (para. 1)

According to Woodard (2016), the scuffle between individual rights and the good of the community rests at the intersection of almost every single principal dispute in American history. And it seems, by design, that individual rights always draw the short stick. Individual rights or human rights all suffer the same fate, lip service.

Repucci and Slipowitz (2021) noted that not adhering to human rights standards is "shifting the international balance in favor of tyranny" (p. 1). This failure to adhere to human rights has resulted in the "15th consecutive year of decline in global freedom" (Repucci & Slipowitz, 2021, p. 1). With the deterioration in global freedom, Amnesty International (2021) informed the General Assembly of the Organization of American States (OAS), an international body which the United States is a member state, that "they need to seek comprehensive solutions to the historic and structural problems of the region, focusing their efforts on guaranteeing and respecting human rights" (para. 1).

At the Summit for Democracy, President Biden (2021) told world leaders that "we have to stand for justice and the rule of law, for free speech, free assembly, a free press, freedom of religion, and for all the inherent human rights of every individual" (para. 19).

On the other side of the world, French President Emmanuel Macron (as cited in British Broadcasting Corporation (BBC), 2022) said "I really want to piss them [the unvaccinated] off, and we'll carry on doing this - to the end" (para. 1). President Macron's view is that life should be dismal for all the unvaccinated (Breeden, 2022). President Macron is only expressing what many democratic governments, including the French policies they are practicing against their people, are executing. Remember, France is a democratic country and the unvaccinated have not committed any criminal offenses. Unfortunately, the level of invective, microaggression, and vitriol being spewed for the unvaccinated leads to violence against the unvaccinated both from state and private actors.

It gets complicated when those sworn to uphold the people's human rights and constitutional rights violate them. It gets even dicier when the person we helped elect is the perpetrator who violates our human and constitutional rights. Politicians can bring democracies to the brink of no repair. According to Levitsky and Ziblatt (2018):

> It is less dramatic but equally destructive. Democracies may die at the hands not of generals but of elected leaders—presidents and prime ministers who subvert the very process that brought them to power. Some of these leaders dismantle democracy quickly, as Hitler did in the wake of the 1933 Reichstag fire in Germany. More often, though, democracies erode slowly, in barely visible steps. (p. 3)

Many people saw President Trump and his behaviors as a destructive device dismantling Democracies, and he was. M. Wolff (2021) said that "Trump's true assault on democratic norms was to have moved organization, strategy, method, rationale, and conscious decision making from the highest level of government" (p. xiv).

But while President Trump was responsible for many issues, he was not solely responsible for any one single issue. Singling out Trump and not others, including the broader issues that brought society to this point, is counterproductive (Hedges, 2010). Tavernise (2021) summed it up this way: "From lockdowns to masks to vaccines to school curriculums, the conflicts in America keep growing and morphing, even without Donald Trump" (para. 8).

When one takes off the chocolate-covered glasses (i.e., our implicit biases), they will find some of the most destructive elected leaders to Democracy are the cunning and baffling, not to mention the charismatics. This includes how politicians handle the COVID-19 pandemic. To date, amid a pandemic, we have seen some of the most aberrant and destructive human rights and inalienable rights violations known to humankind.

The worst irony of the COVID-19 pandemic is that "some of the most abrupt reversals [in the stance on inalienable rights and human rights] are occurring in countries where the laws and culture cherish the sanctity of personal rights" (Landler, 2021, para. 3).

Unfortunately, the track record of COVID-19 violations includes the termination of the unvaccinated (Slotnik, 2021), the house arrest of the unvaccinated (Eddy, 2021), the levying of fines against unvaccinated seniors (60 years of age or older) (Gatopoulos, 2022), the placement in internment camps of the unvaccinated (Cave, 2021), the censorship of data (Tyson et al., 2022), the public shaming of people (Gan, 2021), the severe restrictions on the movements and social life of the unvaccinated (Schuetze, 2021b, 2021a), general lockdowns (Onyeaka et al., 2021), and use of batons and dogs to break up COVID-19 public gatherings (Reuters, 2022). Onyeaka et al. (2021) noted that at a minimum, five pandemics have occurred from 2009 to 2019 without lockdowns and none meriting lockdowns.

Israel's Coronavirus Czar, Dr. Salman Zarka (as cited in Tercatin, 2021) said that forced house arrests on the unvaccinated are improper and that such practices may have triggered a slippery slope. In other words, the entire world is watching, and everyone is looking for fresh ideas to copy and paste for the COVID-19 pandemic.

When politicians claim they are following science, Austria is a prime example of politicians saying one thing but doing another. According to Iversen (as cited in Hill, 2021), the Austrian Minister, Wolfgang Mückstein, had recommended a general lockdown before the implementation of the house arrest on the unvaccinated, but Chancellor Karl Nehammer pursued a different agenda, locking down the unvaccinated. Regrettably, many politicians who claim to follow science deploy this approach as a comfort device. Austrian politicians are not the only ones practicing Machiavellian communications. Democracies worldwide, through their elected officials, are exercising the use of comfort devices while simultaneously seeking the same or similar agendas as Austria but often with a much subtler approach.

Austria placed the unvaccinated on house arrest, but in reality, lockdowns, according to Berenson (2021), have accomplished more destruction than the construction of our norms, rights, and standards, which "in our desperation to control COVID-19, we had done more damage to ourselves and the world [through the diminution of rights and the way of life] than the virus ever could" (p. 1). This speaks to what Strauss and Howe (2009) noted concerning parents' fear about the American Dream dissipating, saying that the dream "was there (solidly) for their parents and still there (barely) for them, [but] will not be there for their kids" (p. 1).

With the prospect of the American Dream seemingly dissolving for many, it is mind-bending, just baffling to observe how other health practitioners respond differently than those healthcare professionals charged with the care of the American people. For example, Israel's Public Health Services lead, Dr. Sharon Alroy-Preis (as cited in Tercatin, 2021) noted that Israel has approached the COVID-19 pandemic not by categorizing it as an emergency but a concerning situation demanding a rapid response that they do not desire to turn into an emergency. This approach is in stark contrast to the targeted fearmongering that has continued in the United States since March 2020.

In the case of *County of Butler, at al. v. Thomas W. Wolf at al. No: 2:20-cv-677* (2020) Judge William Shaw Stickman, IV noted that "lockdowns have never been used for any other disease in our [the United States] history" (p. 44). Judge Stickman noted that communist China, a country unconstricted by civil liberties, constitutional rights, human rights, or any other right triggered a domino effect, which has since been copied and pasted throughout the world (*County of Butler, at al. v. Thomas W. Wolf at al. No: 2:20-cv-677*, 2020). It seems China has contributed more than COVID-19 to the world, and despots seem to copy and paste this infectious brand of communism throughout the world wittingly or unwittingly, but as will be seen more wittingly.

Judge Stickman noted that:
The liberties protected by the Constitution are not fare-weather freedoms—in place when times are good but able to be cast aside in times of trouble. There is no question this country has faced, and will face, emergencies of every sort. But the solution to a national crisis

6

can never be permitted to supersede the commitment to individual liberty that stands as the foundation of the American experiment. (*County of Butler, at al. v. Thomas W. Wolf at al. No: 2:20-cv-677,* 2020, pp. 65–66)

Rejecting the conquest of Casanova is not easy. Greene and Elffers (2003) noted that Casanova was "the most successful seducer in history" ("The Romantic Ideal," para. 9). Hence, *despite what politicians may say on social media or national television, we must not be drawn by the honey of their lips but by the understanding of what they are willing to place their wet-ink signatures on or cast their binding votes toward.* The same thing applies to corporate CEOs. But of course, politicians and CEOs know, as noted by Benoit (1997) that "perceptions are more important than reality" (p. 178).

Despite whatever side of the COVID-19 pandemic divide, one stands, our rights have slid down the slippery slope of no return. And when the dust settles, the new world order will have emerged, and the people of the United States will have no one else to blame but themselves. When the COVID-19 pandemic is finally declared over, we will have collectively done more damage to the American people economically and psychologically than every war since World War I (WWI). Ferguson (2008) and McMeekin (2014) both discuss the carnage of WWI.

In the case, Dr. A. et al. v. Kathy Hochul, Governor of New York, et al. 595 U. S. _____ (2021) (cert. denied), Justice Gorsuch documented that Governor Kathy Hochul issued a vaccine mandate without a religious exemption after the state had informed people the mandate would have an exception, yet when the mandate was issued, it did not contain the promised religious exception.

Governor Hochul was just elevated to the position of governor, and this is a poor way to make an initial impression. These postures are representative of the spiritual blackout within the United States. While Justice Gorsuch noted New York had "backtracked" (p. 1), backtracking seems to be common today when it comes to inalienable and constitutional rights. According to the International Institute for Democracy and Electoral Assistance (2021), "backsliding are found in some of the world's largest countries," including the United States (p. 1).

If the Constitution could be thrown away right now, some of the very elected or in the case of Governor Hochul, selected would shred the Constitution. What stands out most about this case is the fact that Justice

Gorsuch noted that Governor Hochul said that "no 'organized religion' sought it [i.e., the religious exemption] and individuals who did were not 'listening to God and what God wants' (*Dr. A. et al. v. Kathy Hochul, Governor of New York, et al. 595 U. S. _____ (cert. denied)*, 2021, p. 1). Governor Hochul's view suggests she is king, priest, and prophet, and this is expressly what the United States Constitution prohibits.

Governor Hochul, in her proper person and representative of the people, shows pompous indignation, unspeakable before the pandemic. Unless everyone attends "the Church of New York State," everyone else's religious expression is meaningless under Governor Hochul's actions and views, the state-sanctioned religion. Governor Hochul's view is from a "palace of crystals" (Dostoevsky, 2021, p. 1851).

Justice Gorsuch also noted that Governor Hochul does attend church, noting that she explained: "How can you believe that God would give a vaccine that would cause you harm? That is not truth. Those are just lies out there on social media" (*Dr. A. et al. v. Kathy Hochul, Governor of New York, et al. 595 U. S. _____ (cert. denied)*, 2021, p. 4).

There are three fundamental things wrong with Governor Hochul's assertion of which I will simply point to the most basic: anyone who attends a church knows basic familiarity with God is an individual experience. The COVID-19 pandemic has shown the world if they are listening, politicians will say anything and do anything.

As corporations observe the backsliding by the United States government and many state governments, they seem to have been greenlighted for the same type of practices within their organization, leading to the basic problem.

The Problem

You made your bed hard. Now, you have to sleep in it. —Katie Ricks McCastle

Companies have implemented, at a record pace, seemingly impenetrable COVID-19 vaccination policies in a bandwagon-like pattern, sweeping across the United States in clock-work order. According to Harris (2021), a slew of U.S. organizations, at present, have or will force their employees to become vaccinated against COVID-19. Under this regime, terminating unvaccinated employees has become ostensibly commonplace and fashionable (A. Smith, 2021). The unvaccinated appear to have become the universal scapegoat as this practice reverberates across the United States. In past epidemics or pandemics, blaming others, microaggression, and full-on violence was common and well documented (Harsh, 2020).

Terminations are adding up, fast. The jagged consequences await the terminated, unvaccinated after being ripped from their roles within organizations (A. Smith, 2021). However, outside of the United States, compelled vaccination for employees was nearly unheard of, and such practices were legally barred (Ratcliffe & Wilson, 2021). Then again, legal thresholds in the COVID-19 world seem to amount to something imaginary and change on a whim. For example, even some European countries are now imposing no health pass, no paycheck-style policies (New York Times, 2021), following in the steps of the United States.

Europe had resisted the same maladroit, COVID-19 approach practiced in the United States, but under pressure have succumbed to end COVID-19 swiftly. In the end, fear was weaponized to reach the United Kingdom's desired effect (Dodsworth, 2021). McDonald (2021) noted that when fear becomes pathologic, fear injures individuals, and it damages families and communities. Global anxiety from perceived or real lackluster COVID-19 responses can be traced back to rational fear (Faranda, 2020). "We act (learn, remember, crave, attach) in relation to fear, or surprise, enjoyment, or shame" (Frank & Wilson, 2020, "Drives," para. 3). When fear becomes unbridled, it turns into a deceptive tool with which no one can harness its properties. It can get out of control, fast.

COVID-19, however, seems to be endemic (Mandavilli, 2022c; Meredith, 2021; K. Miller, 2021), here for a while, especially with its continued mutations: Delta and Omicron. Christakis (2020) had predicted a second COVID-19 wave. But now, the world has found itself in the clutches of the third wave of COVID-19.

The expectation has shifted to an enduring COVID-19 pandemic which will not end in the virus fading away from interfering with public life; however, as an alternative, the hope is that when a sufficient level of people gain immunity, such protection will lower COVID-19's spread and decrease hospitalizations and deaths, even while COVID-19 circulates and lingers (Feldscher, 2021). Whatever hope that had existed that COVID-19 would magically disappear is sharply misguided (Atlas, 2021). And this misguided approach set the American peoples' expectations so high, and so unbelievable, that it set them up for failure.

Unfortunately, according to Dr. Céline Gounder (as cited in Amanpour and Company, 2021), "herd immunity is off the table" (section, 10:10 – 10:13). Immunity for the herd is "now just a dream" (Mandavilli, 2022c, para. 9), a pipedream. Sadly, COVID-19 will continue to fluctuate (Atlas, 2021). With herd immunity off the table, Levin-Scherz and Toro (2021) recommended that employers must remain up to date on the efficacy of current interventions.

And even if COVID-19 were eradicated today, that would not unring the bell of the economic, social, political, and physical problems that arose from the pandemic. Hence, public policy issues would still abound (Feldscher, 2021). Delavega (2021) noted, for example, that the COVID-19 pandemic economic pain impacted the hardest on the lower echelon of society.

If the no health pass, no paycheck-style or no jab, no job policies receive the full faith and credit these practices are designed to accomplish, this means every country's government whose implementation or allowed such implementation would endorse and follow a practice of starvation of its people. Choose your own bodily integrity and starve. Starvation is more painful than burning and gassing.

Take, for example, New York City, according to Cooper (2021), mayor Bill De Blasio announced a city-wide universal vaccine mandate. De Blasio (as cited in Cooper, 2021) said:

> The more universal they are, the more likely employees will say okay, it's time. I'm going to do this. Because you can't jump from one industry to another or one company to another. It's something that needs to be universal to protect all of us. (para. 4)

De Blasio also said:

> The key is more, more, and more vaccinations. So we are going to implement these mandates aggressively. We're sending out inspectors, we need people to do this, we need all of these mandates to be followed. The more we vaccinate, the more we can get through this and the great danger here is shutdowns and restrictions. (Eyewitness News, 2021)

When you start with a sledgehammer like De Blasio, there are no other options available to him other than greater government intervention and force. If the key is more vaccination, then how come New York added a record number of 22,000 positive COVID-19 cases on December 18,

2021. And one of the things I have learned in law enforcement, the more force you use, the more attention comes and the more problems.

Should De Blasio and others keep pushing such a flawed notional approach to vaccines, when an effective vaccine is correctly developed, The American people will have become overcome with vaccine fatigue. Pandemic fatigue has already begun to set in from mismatched and often confusing information (Mazzei, 2021).

According to David (2021b), "the Omicron wave is exposing the limits of COVID-19 restrictions, which are clearly failing" (para. 2). Indeed. Unfortunately, many businesses and employees, especially the unvaccinated, terminated employees bore and continue to bear "the brunt of questionable protocols that clearly need rethinking, if not scrapping outright" (David, 2021b, para. 3). So, someone needs to quietly tell De Blasio, other state and local government officials, and corporate CEOs that the jig is up; the people know the vaccines are not effective. The answer to this problem will not be found in copying and pasting, lockdowns, or violations of the people's constitutional rights.

In the article, *New York City is being pummeled by Omicron*, Newman (2021) documented the sad truth about De Blasio's failed COVID-19 mandates, noting that "more than 110,000 people have tested positive since Christmas Day, and the positivity rate in some neighborhoods is approaching 30 percent" (para. 5). Even worse, De Blasio unnecessarily spent 10 million dollars to enforce New York City's failed COVID-19 mandate (Fitzsimmons, 2021). With all these failed policies, New York City's health system is once again jammed packed with COVID patients reminiscent of the pandemic's onset in the spring of 2020 (Otterman & Goldstein, 2022).

Earle (2021) noted that "with an effective vaccine, there's no reason to mandate that it be taken" (p. 17). We must stop practicing failed approaches to the COVID-19 pandemic, including the destructive constraints placed upon people, especially the low risk (Atlas, 2021).

CDC Director, Dr. Rochelle Walensky (as cited in Campos, 2021) said that "given the current state of the pandemic, both here and around the world, any vaccination is better than no vaccination" (para. 2). When I read Dr. Walensky's comments, her remarks did not inspire me about the United States' response to COVID-19 because it seems that the government has a spaghetti strategy, throwing anything against the wall, hoping it sticks. Dr. Walensky's statement reminded me of the scene in

Titanic, Cameron (1997) when the ship was going down and the musicians were playing music on the deck.

Many employees opined that vaccine mandates make them believe they are safe (Barry et al., 2021). It is important to note that feeling safe and being safe are two different constructs. Unfortunately, universal mandates always hold untold consequences. For example, David (2021b) noted that "mandates have curbed almost everything except COVID-19 cases" (para. 1). For example, vaccine mandates have increased inflation, left jobs unfilled, and limited the qualified pool of employees (David, 2021a). Consumer prices have not jumped up with this type of intensity since 1982 (Smialek, 2022).

With such high inflation and despite the risk of contaminating coworkers, employees are still showing up to work infected with COVID-19 (Meyersohn, 2022). Showing up to work sick was a common occurrence at the World Bank Group because Allied-Universal Security Services' implementation of inconsistent sick and safe policies. Ultimately, hurtful pre-pandemic practices intensified the risks of COVID-19 in the workplace.

It is the second-order nature of things that rarely, if ever, are shown on the daily news.

The World Health Organization's Europe Director Dr. Hans Kluge (as cited in Ellyatt, 2021) has stepped into the vaccine mandate debate cautioning that obligatory vaccination must be context-specific, saying:

Mandates around vaccination are an absolute last resort, and only applicable when all other feasible options to improve vaccination uptake have been exhausted... The effectiveness of vaccine mandates is very context-specific. The effect mandating vaccines could have on public confidence and public trust, as well as vaccination uptake, must be considered... Ultimately, mandates should never contribute to increasing social inequalities... (paras. 5; 6; 8)

Kennedy (2021) noted that in short order, "liberal democracy effectively collapsed worldwide" (p. 23). Gingrich (2020) explained that over the last six decades, he has not been more concerned for the United States' survival than today. Both Kennedy and Gingrich hold valid concerns because, as Dr. R. D. Wolff (2021) reminded us, the Bubonic plague helped usher in the demise of European feudalism. The Bubonic plague was also responsible for interrupting economic and social life (Lord, 2014). Dr. R. D. Wolff (2021) noted that the capitalist crash was already well overdue, and that COVID-19 only heightened the sickness of the present system.

The system to which Dr. R. D. Wolff (2021) referred to, according to Acemoglu and Robinson (2012), represents "extractive economic institutions—extractive because such institutions are designed to extract incomes and wealth from one subset of society to benefit a different subset of society" (p. 76). While Acemoglu and Robinson look at extractive economic institutions from a monetary standpoint, this view is limited. Extractive economic institutions rob employees of their utility, much broader than monetary value. These extractive economic institutions are not only draining monetary value and utility, but they are also draining employees' life and vitality.

Kennedy (2021) is a staunch liberal and Gingrich (2020) a steadfast conservative, yet they are essentially speaking the same language. Hence, this baffles the mind to see the human rights violations such as denying people's right to earn a living because one's views do not align with a particular ideology.

Denying a person's ability to earn a living because he or she disagrees with the official state position represents an unfathomably masochistic stance, a practice that is antithetical to human rights. Many companies have recognized the problems with the hellish vaccination policies and have begun to promote their companies' no vaccination approach (Whitney, 2021).

Sherfinski (2021) reported that labor unions can negotiate vaccine requirements for employees. From what I have observed, under the labor contract with Allied-Universal Security Services, 32BJ SEIU, and the World Bank Group, the union always capitulates to all the demands of both companies.

The World Bank Group dominates everything. I recall listening to one of the security specialists say to Rick: "Having a union contract is not a requirement to work at the bank." And this is how the World Bank Group responds when it comes to union activity. The World Bank Group does not even allow union activity on their property. The 32BJ SEIU union must meet its members outside of the World Bank Group. Unfortunately, it is this same approach that leads to violations of the peoples' rights.

Denying a person's ability to earn a living represents an eerily similar practice of past despots and tyrants. Lest we forget Adolf Hitler (Germany), Benito Mussolini (Italy), Joseph Stalin (the Soviet Union),

Kim Jong-un (North Korea), Mao Zedong (China), Rodrigo Duterte (the Philippines), Slobodan Milošević (Serbia), to name a few slim despots and tyrants that have ruled major countries.

The critics will argue that I have gone too far, that I do not know what I am talking about, that I am crazy, or even an anti-vaxxer. I do not hang out in anti-vaccination circles or groups. The only thing I am against is autocracy and slavery. If I am accused of anything, fault me for being a lover of the Constitution.

In the book, *Apollo's Arrow: The Profound and Enduring Impact of Coronavirus on the Way We Live*, Christakis (2020) noted that "many people believe that the efforts to contain the virus have been excessive" ("Preface," para. 4). Consider me one of those people who believe the efforts have been overly broad and detrimental to fundamental rights. Christakis (2020) chalks up others' perspectives as "wrong thinking," noting that it has taken all our technical and medical advances to limit deaths to current levels ("Preface," para. 4). Christakis' point of view here assumes that the actors (i.e., businesses and governments) had good intentions and maintained good intentions throughout the COVID-19 pandemic.

I refused to be taken by the long con, which according to Pace (2015), represents a "slow, drawn-out method of persuasion" (p. 30). And I simply am not going to be brainwashed, which K. Taylor (2017) described as "controlling people's beliefs so effectively that they do not feel manipulated—as if the imposed beliefs were their own" (p. ix).

Despots understand that people require "miracle [economic power—bread], mystery [psychological power], and authority [political power]" (Dostoyevsky, 2012, p. 22; *The Holy Bible, New King James Version*, 1982, Chapter Matthew 4:1-11), the consolation for humans in periods of protracted fear and uncertainty (Dalton, 2013). Hence, critical thinkers are a threat to authority and the status quo (Bell Hooks, 2014), because the masses are supposed to be passive spectators for the higher echelon (Chomsky, 2015). And therefore, dark psychology and persuasion are used by corporate and government actors, frequently.

Corporations and the United States government are practicing dark psychology and dark persuasion, and completely manipulated the science that I love. Corporate interests are unbelievably embedded in science (Mikovits et al., 2020). Science has gone from public interest to private interest. This manipulation of the people adds to what Saad (2020) noted as the degradation of humans' ability to think critically which forms "a collective malady that destroys people's capacity to think rationally" (p. XI).

And in the trail of tears left behind in the aftermath of the COVID-19 pandemic, many will discover that they have been victims of a strong-arm robbery, but not with hands, fists, or feet. The people will discover that they have been the subject of "human hacking" (Hadnagy, 2018, p. 9; Hadnagy & Schulman, 2021, p. 3).

Human hacking can ensure that "new ideas may be implanted and firmly fixed in the minds even of those unwilling at first to receive them" (Sargant & Swencionis, 2019, p. xxi). Marine Corps, Colonel Frank H. Schwable (as cited in Meerloo, 2015) described it this way:

The words were mine... the thoughts were theirs. That is the hardest thing I have to explain: how a man can sit down and write something he knows is false, and yet, to sense it, to feel it, to make it seem real. (p. 10)

Governments and individuals who practice mind control (i.e., coercive persuasion) follow the perspective of Gardner (2006), who offered this advice: "It is to spend less time trying to convince individuals of a new perspective, and more time trying to understand and thereby to neutralize the resistance" ("Preface," para. 10). Since brainwashing, conditioning, and indoctrination began, the tools of the trade have sharply developed.

Current practices of mind control center around developing habits. People are corralled into the habit zone and peppered with mental triggers (Eyal, 2014). In the habit zone, actions are performed, variable rewards are offered, and uninformed investments are churned out (Eyal, 2014; University of California Television (UCTV), 2017).

Mind control and influence operations are always updated and refined.

According to Winn (2011), the Chinese regularly deployed mind control tactics. Meerloo (2015) called it "political conditioning" (p. 32). And after much time studying thought reform (mind control), it is a noticeable influence that slowly encroaches on the people, which Lifton (2012) said mind control may be "the most dangerous direction of the twentieth-century mind—the quest for absolute or 'totalistic' belief systems" (p. vii).

Whether one believes in mind control or not, Psychiatrist, Dr. Dimsdale (2021) noted that there are practices that can be applied to leave people exposed to the mental control of others. Wegner (1989) said that "we do not seem to have much control over our minds" (p. vii). One form of these practices is designed by what Johnson (2021) called "choice architecture" (p. 2). Another of these practices is employed in mind control stems from what Thaler and Sunstein (2021) called "nudging" (p. xiv). Nostalgia provides another avenue for brainwashing (Lindstrom & Spurlock, 2011).

A simple example of mind control at work would include the view that one's colleague is lazy. Price (2021) noted that thinking people are lazy is part of a larger lie people have been spoon-fed. What happens when people think of others as lazy or themselves as lazy, they try to work even harder, believing their worth is earned through productivity or you may treat your colleague differently after thinking he or she is lazy (Price, 2021). Americans are some of the hardest working people on the planet, and the only people benefiting from the laziness lie are corporations and the United States government. Ultimately, mind control and manipulation occur through the blurring of the lines between what something is and what something is not (Lustig, 2017).

Many people believe that they can use willpower to overcome psychological manipulation, they are wrong. And a failure to properly understand this concept can set the stage for "ego depletion" (Baumeister & Tierney, 2011, p. 31). Wegner (1989) said it this way: "When we admonish ourselves not to do something, not to believe something, not to feel something, even not to think something, our attempt to say no is often no more effective than a flyswatter held up to stop a cannonball" (p. vii). The ones practicing mind control understand how to exert influence to overcome resistance.

Hardy (2018) noted that "if you're required to exert willpower to do something, there is an obvious internal conflict" (Willpower Doesn't Work," para. 1). Accordingly, manipulation is only overcome by developing an internal capacity to fend off psychological intrusions.

Without the internal capacity to fend off manipulation, the robbers will make a clean get-a-way. When the people discover what was stolen, they will find that they have been robbed of their constitutional rights along with their ability to think critically through a manage by crisis approach.

16

The reason mind control is important is that as Halperin (2015) noted, social and moral wrongdoing is perfected in peace rather than violence, and peace is the preferred method of most people. This is partially why management by crisis and fear approaches are often the dominant approach.

In this cyclical management by crisis strategy, corporations and governments always follow crisis communications and never miss opportunities to use bolstering (i.e., stress the good) or minimization (i.e., an act is less serious) tactics (Benoit, 1997). What happens is people make decisions primarily based on fear. According to McDonald (2021), anytime fear becomes a primary object in the decision-making process, the quality of such decisions always deteriorates. Fear can be so complete that it overtakes all other emotions in the human body (G. de Becker, 1997).

According to Meerloo (2015), "if we are to survive as free men, we must face up to this problem of politically inspired mental coercion with all its ramifications" (p. 10). Failure to understand the ramifications of political mental coercion will render the people prisoners of deceit.

Prisoners of deceit watch movies such as *In Time*, Niccol (2011), *The Matrix*, Wachowski and Wachowski (1999), and *Soylent Green*, Fleischer (1973) for their entertainment value, and that is fine, but they truly misunderstand what is truly communicated. The movie *In Time* depicts the American caste system. While *The Matrix* is more intricate, one of the underlying themes of the movie is the mind control of the people. *Soylent Green* is a 1973 movie set in the City of New York in the year 2022 that addresses government and corporate collusion that influences public policy decisions of major national importance. Today, all these issues influence the COVID-19 response.

I am not the first to understand and link these types of measures to past despots and tyrants. For example, Horowitz and Martin (2018) showed that the World Health Organization (WHO) was conducting identical experimentation as Adolf Hitler had done through the medical experimentation of people. Japanese doctors had also conducted similar unethical experiments like those authorized by Adolf Hitler (Spitz, 2005).

Understanding history is an essential bulwark against totalitarianism, a subject to which violators of human rights do not want the masses to understand. According to Piketty (2020), "a historical understanding remains our best tool" against the foes of human rights (p. 2). We do not fully appreciate history because it is too easy to be dismissed by fake news and alternative facts.

When I began writing my Ph.D. dissertation, I stumbled onto two interesting concepts on why people are so easily bamboozled: "shifting baseline syndrome" (SBS) (Pierce, 2020, para. 1) and "environmental generational amnesia" (EGA) (Peter H. Kahn & Thea Weiss, 2017, p. 8; University of Washington, 2017). They just move the goal post, and the unsuspecting can never even develop a clue something is wrong. Therefore, there are so many questions that require candid and truthful answers.

Lauren (2013) asked a poignant question: "Why [do] the rights of men appear to be so meaningless to those who so deliberately violated them" ("Lecture 1: The Rights of Man," section, 3:43)? It is to this question that Becker and Keen (2007) noted that one's desire for the best can ultimately drive the worst.

Talk About Trickle Down

Long-term thinking protects us during downturns (of all kinds), because it keeps us moving toward our most important goals. —
Dorie Clark

There are always secondary, tertiary, and quadrilateral problems following major incidents of a financial crisis, natural disaster, and war. These problems plague the nightly news in many media markets, and such incidents often leave communities paralyzed for years or decades trying to recover from the ills of the initial incident. It is too easy to focus on issues such as the Great Depression (1929 - 1933), Hurricane Katrina (2005), or the 2008 financial crisis. Those events are low-hanging fruit. All the mentioned events are instructive, but there is still something missing, the aftermath.

Looking at the aftermath can tell us a lot about the current and future aftermath of the COVID-19 pandemic. Much attention can go into an initial event, and this attention can also serve as a distraction to collateral events.

It is understood that distraction is wired into the human condition (Jackson & McKibben, 2008), and has been noted as a "crisis of attention" (Crawford, 2015, "Preface," para. 1). Even worse, Hallowell

(2014) noted that distraction will continue nipping away at human attention while also growing exponentially. And the lack of attention and distraction provides corporations and governments the tacit occasion to squeeze people, to change rules, and to manipulate.

Take, for example, the stock market crash of 1929. Indeed, the market crash was a horrible, no-good event for the bankers who played the game, but even worse for the non-bankers. The Great Depression was a bleak time for Americans who experienced it. While morgues may have held bodies after people lost their livelihood, the individuals most affected were people being treated for mental health issues, having to stand in breadlines for meals, and the new occupants of 'Hoovervilles,' in today's vernacular, skid row (Lowenthal, 1987, para. 8).

In the book, *Fear: Anti-Semitism in Poland after Auschwitz*, Gross (2007) noted that after WWII was well over, the Poles, whom the Nazis considered subhuman and only useful for physical labor, cheated, looted, murdered, plundered, and robbed Jewish people in Poland. Think about this. The same people Hitler trained his turret of indiscriminate hardship for physical labor were the same people who continued the reign of terror on Jewish people.

It is also important to know that, in the aftermath of things, sometimes people keep fighting, such is the case in Berlin, Germany 1944 after America had captured the city (Jähner, 2022). It took another six months for WWII to be declared complete.

In another example, the year 2005 was devastating to Louisiana. Hurricane Katrina brought devastation like no other before or since to the shores of New Orleans, "the Big Easy". When Hurricane Katrina breached New Orleans' infrastructure a chain of events cascaded that no one understood at the time.

Of course, people knew that New Orleans should be evacuated, they knew that before the storm. What was not expected was the disenfranchisement of a city (the entire city) and its people by the same people assigned to help. Did I mention the city?

To place the aftermath of Hurricane Katrina in context, the privileged and the underprivileged were both screwed, although the privileged fared much better off afterward.

There is one Hurricane Katrina story that I would like to share. Above everything that I know about the events of Hurricane Katrina, one event stands saliently above all others in my mind: the Danziger Bridge shooting.

As we continue to experience the effects of the COVID-19 pandemic, the Danziger Bridge shooting represents the same type of emotions and environment that allowed those police officers to raise the business end of their service weapons, shooting six unarmed people (Grimm, 2015).

The Danziger Bridge shooting occurred nearly a week after Hurricane Katrina's devastation. Unfortunately, it is now 22 months after the initial COVID-19 response and the same fear and do-whatever tactics still abound.

Many would observe the facts of the Danziger Bridge shooting and believe it was just the squad of police officers who shot those people, and they did, but the system also pulled the trigger. The government's approach and willingness to say anything and do anything a week after the initial aftermath of Hurricane Katrina highlights the main perpetrator of the Danziger Bridge shooting. The same say anything and do anything strategy has crept into the COVID-19 pandemic response.

In the book, *The Great Crash 1929*, Galbraith and Galbraith (2009) walked through how the American people were fleeced by the bankers and that the United States government knew what to do in 1929, and again in 2008, but failed both times. *The American people have become unwitting stooges, pawns in an American caste, shackled by insurmountable debt, and chained to unscrupulous employers.*

In my life, I have always operated under the impression that people much older than I possess a breadth and depth of experience that I could admire and learn from. President Biden is much older than I am, and he comes with much more experience than I have, and in fact, all the governors of the several states are much older than I am too. So, my question is why, with all the experience and resources at their disposal of the American people, would they allow the United States to disintegrate into the chaos that it has because of COVID-19? Is there no voice of reason? No, that is not the answer.

The American people are being fleeced again. Again!

DeChalus et al. (2021) reported that at least 75 lawmakers hold or have held an interest in vaccine manufacturers. DeChalus et al. only reported lawmakers for the federal government. When the damage is finally completed and comprehended, the American people will have found that not only federal policymakers but also state and local leaders have direct links to the vaccine manufacturers to benefit from the pandemic off the backs of the American people. In law, the concept is called unclean hands. These people have unclean hands as they force these vaccine mandates on the American people to push corporate stock prices up for these vaccine manufacturers.

As DeChalus et al.'s (2021) story get more complicated and when the dust settles, the American people will have found corporate America is also playing the game too, and this includes members of the media. While the American people were being forced back to the office through vaccine mandates, the American people will find the fat cats got richer while the American people became poorer, just fleeced.

Talk About a Pandemic

When we go through hard times, we are able
to stretch and develop. —Tracy Brower

Employees have experienced a series of pandemics which include pandemics of social injustice (Garrick, 2012; Lind & Tyler, 2013), glass ceilings (Pietrangelo, 2020), sticky floors (Shambaugh, 2007), pay inequality (Jones, 2021; Patten, 2016), discrimination (Avery & Ruggs, 2020), delayed retirement (E. Hubler, 1999; Sommer, 2002), and depleted pension plans (Comen, 2019).

The COVID-19 pandemic has fueled what D. Bhanot et al. (2021) styled as "othering" (para. 1). The othering has driven large-scale stigmatization against individuals, groups, and nations, pitting individuals against individuals, groups against groups, and nations against nations.

Now, employees can add COVID-19's posterior effects such as mass termination to the accumulated pain meted out by American organizations.

Lenderman and Langham (2019) noted that employees epitomize organizations' single most indispensable resource. Yet, *the COVID-19 approach pushed down by many corporations treated terminated, unvaccinated employees materially different, reducing the unvaccinated to nothingness, not even the dirty gum under one's shoe.*

After employees have waited, following building closures resulting from COVID-19 restrictions, the terminated, unvaccinated employees had to address the dread of receiving a pink slip, chopped down like trees because they chose their own bodily integrity over what the masses have desired.

Even under these circumstances and high uncertainty, some employees may still present with high levels of optimism, believing they are less likely to experience a negative event (Sweeny & Shepperd, 2007a). As the moment of truth approaches, however, Sweeny et al. (2006) noted that shifts in optimism occur. And then, the sledgehammer drops, employers announce to their employees, get vaccinated, or be terminated.

The binary option, get vaccinated or be terminated, triggers negative emotions especially at the beginning of the announcement (Sweeny & Andrews, 2014), one to which employees would just rather get it over with (Sun et al., 2015).

Even worse, when a negative funk occurs, perceived time factors (i.e., the slowness of the event) can also heighten the terminated, unvaccinated employees' distress (Santoro, 2021). Accordingly, the time between the announced COVID-19 mitigation plans and the waiting period between termination harms employees' health, simply because having to wait on the negative information, the termination (Howell & Sweeny, 2016). Considering this information, it is important to note, the brain is "always listening and responding to hidden influences that act on it" (Amen, 2021, p. 2). The negative information, in this instance, termination, adds to what the terminated, unvaccinated employee would be considered unfair, and unjust behavior within the workplace triggers social stress, which can generate depressive symptoms (Schonfeld et al., 2017).

Most times, employers do not consider all the facets of what is being communicated when they inform someone they will be terminated. Essentially, employers communicate that they are stripping employees of their identity, friendships, self-worth, personal fulfillment, and one's ability to earn a living.

Even further, Schonfeld et al. (2017) noted that unemployment steals the jobless' psychological health by denying the prospects to gain at work, disconnecting the capacity to share experiences (with family and others), eliminating exchanges with persons outside one's household, detaching time structure, and reducing characteristic activity. Remove all these activities and features away at once, while also dealing with a pandemic, and organizations create deep water waves for the terminated, unvaccinated employees. That is, the bad news triggers an "emotional wave" (Birkel & Miller, 1998, p. 49).

Such an emotional wave comes because termination and unemployment, according to Van Horn (as cited in Pappas, 2020), come with "psychological trauma" and "financial trauma" (para. 4). Pappas (2020) summed it up, noting that "losing one's job is detrimental to mental health —and often physical health—even without serious financial strain" (para. 5). And here is the kicker: According to DiGangi (2021), emotional pain is more pertinent to people than physical pain, not only because something hurts but also because the pain becomes wedged into one's memory, developing into living memory. However, Rego (2021) noted that mental pain may meet with a customary low ranking over physical pain because of cultural loading and assigning values and virtues such pain does not hold.

At this point, all types of biological and psychological responses occur, but commonly the terminated, unvaccinated would generally experience loss and grief, the biological response is fear (from the carrot and stick), which leads to fight, flight, freeze, tend, or befriend responses from employees. "The pandemic has wrought grief and trauma, and the introspection it has prompted has exposed our fragility" (Chatterjee, 2021, para. 2).

According to Crouse et al. (2021), society has experienced a collective loss, and because of the loss, we are collectively experiencing both ambiguous loss and ambiguous grief for things and people, including what we did not have or experience. Society has woke up to the idea of ambiguous losses experienced in life (Bernhard, 2021; Boss, 2021). While some losses may be uniquely personal, there are collective losses experienced such as loss of freedom, loss of employment, loss of a sense of safety to name a few (Pentaris, 2021). All these losses trigger so many untold stories of grief.

Grief responses to loss may include anger, denial, or shock, to name some emotions (Kubler-Ross & Kessler, 2005). Grief always begins from the ordinary nature of things (Didion, 2020). Anxiety, frustration, stress, and regret are key signatures of employee termination, because, according to Fullenkamp (2015), many bad things appear to take place without warning.

The Bad News of a Termination

Our painful experiences aren't a liability—
they're a gift. They give us perspective and
meaning, an opportunity to find our unique
purpose and our strength. —Edith Eger

One of the goals of providing bad news is that employees grasp and retain information regarding the bad news and the consequences of the bad news (Sweeny & Shepperd, 2007b). Who in the hell does not understand the consequences of a binary choice: get vaccinated or be terminated. Your entire life now becomes a clock, *a ticking life bomb.*

The terminated, unvaccinated employees begin to question him- or herself. "I thought we have constitutional rights." "I live in a free country." "I gave this employer my life." "I put up with all the bull from this employer and now they're doing this to me." These sentiments represent some of the triggered thoughts from the raw emotions that arrive when trying to navigate the corporate setting.

Many of these emotions are often easily dismissed in a system to which we find ourselves working.

These feelings surface from life's regret, the failure to accept responsibility and take charge of your own life. And when we fail to take charge of our own life, Ware (2019) noted that the number one regret people hold is: "I wish I'd had the courage to live a life true to myself, not the life others expected of me" (p. 44).

Although termination is a painful experience, sending an employee into emotional waves, people, according to Bonanno (2021), can often resume their somewhat routine lives swiftly. Those employees are the people who, according to Kabat-Zinn (2013), "ride the wave" (p. 70). In this case, this would mean getting back in the workforce, but with companies upholding vaccination policies, normal seems to be a longshot for the unvaccinated. The underlying problem here is that employees would be too busy licking their wounds and have no room to manage anything else, including healing (Boyes, 2015).

More Bad News

Sucking it up at the job you hate won't make it
more enjoyable. —Mary Hoang

In the epigraph, it was noted that the industrious must be first to taste from the field of his or her labor. The reason employees have been denied first dibs today results from a lack of ownership of our own field. There is a myriad of issues that may have driven a lack of owning our own fields but here is one take.

According to Slater (2016), people "put a lot of energy into creating and re-creating the social calamities that oppress, infuriate, and exhaust us" ("I Only Work Here," para. 4). While some were busy oppressing themselves, others had simply failed to understand the rules of the game. Two types of games exist: finite and infinite (Carse, 2011; Sinek, 2019). And in this failure to understand the rules of the game, corporations have systematically used our language—vis-à-vis happiness and success—to steamroll their employees.

Employees are supposed to be stakeholders of an organization. "A stakeholder is any group or individual who can affect, or is affected by the achievements of a corporation's purpose" (Freeman, 2010, "Preface," para. 4) But employees, through the diminution of power and socioeconomic advantage, received such a de minimis value, it does not seem to matter what organizations do to employees. That is, the asymmetrical corporate environment has sought to diminish the normal give and take relationship between organizations and employees, forcing employees into a contraflow type situation where such a workforce cannot influence corporations through business adhesion.

In my undergraduate study, I read a book called, *Life Launch: A Passionate Guide to the Rest of Your Life*. After reading the book, I could never forget this quote, which F. M. Hudson and McLean (2006) said:

> If you refuse to initiate your own path, your choice will be the leftovers from those around you who did entrepreneur their futures, and put you to work for their destinies... If you don't know where you're going, anywhere will do, and the push-pull of life around you will shape your push—to somewhere you haven't chosen but have to adjust to. (pp. 4-5)

Under this same toxic regime, organizations know and have known, publicly, for at least 11 years that the lack of social relationship holds the same health risk of mortality that is associated with cigarettes (Holt-Lunstad et al., 2010), with some guesstimating as high as 15 cigarettes a day (Franke, 2021; McGregor, 2017). Still, organizations use just-in-time hiring methods where employees get insufficient preparation and are ousted without regard for their medical and psychological care.

Employees are operating from leftovers, the scraps to which these organizations determine their worthiness. Employees are clocking in and clocking out daily, working for the corporate stockholders' destinies, not their own. Employees consistently adjusted their lives for the corporate vulture only to find, their efforts would be greeted with no gratitude. And after being chewed up and drained of their utility, the terminated, unvaccinated employees were determined unworthy, even unfit for the scraps. Sadly, this is the organizational culture to which these corporations perpetuate.

Organizational Culture

The thorn from the bush one has planted, nourished, and pruned, pricks most deeply and draws more blood. —Maya Angelou

An issue many organizations experience, they fail to understand their own organizational culture (which occurs at the unit level). The culture of an organization flows in a bidirectional manner from the top and the bottom, from leadership's vision and employees' collective experiences brought into an organization (Armstrong & Mitchell, 2019).

Vanderbloeme (2018) noted that discovering culture is essential because *if an organization has a bad culture, it wins, every time, and if a company has a great culture, it wins, every time.* If the organizational culture is bad, it is not a big leap to a poor organizational climate (which occurs at the individual level). According to Meyer (2014), an organization's culture can influence what we ascertain, what we reason, and how we behave.

For organizations that selected mass termination as their first and only option, organizational culture, even if such organizations' compensation and fringe benefit package is above average, they operate from poor organizational culture. *Even if corporations with poor organizational cultures desired to hide it, you could not even hide it by camouflaging it.* Your employees know and the people your employees talk to know, and the people they talk to also know.

Organizational culture is associated with organizational performance, recruitment, retention, satisfaction, and well-being, to name some (Jex &

Britt, 2014), and it is difficult for rivals to follow (Heskett, 2022). Part of today's organizational culture hides from the universality of what Singer (2019) called "thinking ethically" (p. 33), which has allowed corporations to run amuck.

With mass termination policies, CEOs failed to assess the psychology of the retained and terminated employees. Ehrenreich (2005) noted that "you don't… have to lose a job to feel the anxiety and despair of the unemployed" (p. 5). Hence, CEOs failed to assess their talent strategy. CEOs failed to build a people approach. And CEOs have failed their people and their organizations.

One would believe that organizations and their leadership would put more thought into their policies and procedures, especially because of the pandemic, before implementing such drastic measures as mass terminations. Unfortunately, it has been common for leaders and managers to latch on to quick fixes (Rosenzweig, 2007). These quick fixes often come at a high cost to their employees and the organizations themselves, leaving a trail of damage in the aftermath of these quick fixes.

For the unvaccinated, terminated employees, we know the outcome of quick fixes. For the clueless, Banaji and Greenwald (2013) noted a sad truth that today, most judgment is compiled with little conscious thought and deliberation. Regrettably, for those organizations, it was just business as usual. But it is not business as usual, we are in a pandemic.

Chapter 2

Copying and Pasting

Copying has been a time-honored means of learning how to do anything. —Gabriella Morrison

Ibarra (2019) noted that many leaders are trying the same things. That is not leadership, and it is far from it. It is copying and pasting.

Hughes et al. (2012) noted that leadership represents a process, and no one needs a position to lead. Leaders are tasked with a few overriding functions such as coordinating and directing the workplace, focusing resources to achieve desired outcomes, and creating conditions for an organization and its employees to be effective, which only name a few (Hughes et al., 2012).

Today's leaders have spent billions of dollars on learning how to become "reflective practitioners" (Schön, 2017, Chapter 2), create "learning organizations" (Senge, 2010, Chapter 1, para. 2), craft "results-based leadership" (Ulrich et al., 1999, p. 19), use "management by objectives" (Drucker, 2008, p. 258), and learn to put "sacred cows" to pasture (Kriegel & Brandt, 1997, p. 1). So, now I am left wondering, how in the hell are all these organizations running the same playbook for a problem that has shown itself to be ineffective on multiple fronts.

COVID-19 has exposed many so-called leaders for what they truly are: parvenus, copying, following, and pasting their way through the business world. It is no wonder organizational change measures fail at over a whopping 70% (Bachmann et al., 2021; Basford & Schaninger, 2016; Shaner, 2010).

Copying and Pasting: The Wuhan Factor

The American people have never been locked down for any other disease in the United States' history. In the spring of 2020, Americans began voluntarily staying home (Zhang, 2021). Voluntary suspension of activities may have resulted from a casualty-focused consciousness (Weitz et al., 2020). Even without such casualty-focused consciousness, people understand the cost of loss, and when such loss becomes inescapable, people make adjustments, unaided (R. Thaler, 1980). Hence, government intervention using stay-at-home orders was overkill and unnecessary.

Stay-at-home orders discounted the human factor. The human factor is this: "Virtually all humans have, for virtually all of recorded history, faced daily risks of disease or violent death that are far greater than those that the residents of developed countries currently face" (Mounk, 2021, para. 17).

California, under Governor Gavin Newsom, is the first state to implement a stay-at-home order (Moreland et al., 2020). If the country continues to follow California, we will all be paying $6.05 per gallon for gasoline, which has reached this amount in California in the pandemic. The only other major government to practice such an approach was the Chinese government in Wuhan, China at the time (*County of Butler, at al. v. Thomas W. Wolf at al. No: 2:20-cv-677*, 2020). In effect, Chinese communist policies and ideologies spread equally fast as the underlying problem, COVID-19.

Governor Newsom copied a communist practice and now, the American people seem not to be able to get rid of such a draconian strategy. *It is like Governor Newsom released a bowl of roaches into the stream of American thought and practices.* And though it seems apparent, it is Democrats willing to follow communist policies and ideologies within the borders of the American shores.

I realize many Republican governors copied what California did in its implementation of COVID-19 lockdowns but many of them were allowed to expire without renewal.

Before the critics accuse me of being partisan, I have been a registered Democrat my entire life. My family and I have voted with the Democratic party on many major issues. I did vote for George W. Bush, however. George W. Bush carries my brand of politics, hard noise, but compassionate. Although I have remained a Democrat, I have voted with Republicans on many issues. Today, however, I am more independent, because the style of politics is too hot on both sides of the aisle.

Outsized Copying and Pasting: The Google Factor

The problem of copying and pasting is widely recognized in business. For example, recently, a group of 600 Google employees disseminated a statement challenging the thoughts behind Google's Covid-19 vaccine mandate (Elias, 2021a). The 600 Google employees noted that the company's COVID-19 approach and "decision will have outsize influence in corporate America" (Elias, 2021a, para. 6). That is, organizations everywhere will copy and paste Google's COVID-19 approach.

Google employees had until December 3, 2021, to declare and disclose their vaccination status or be terminated (Elias, 2021b). Google's employees until January 18, 2022, or they will be placed on 'paid administrative leave' followed by an extended 'unpaid personal leave' and then terminated (Elias, 2021b). The only difference in Google's approach to terminating its unvaccinated employees is whether they will get the fast sledgehammer or the slow sledgehammer. Google's policy is no different from any other vaccination policy, except they may honor medical and religious exemptions.

In his book, *Human Frontiers: The Future of Big Ideas in an Age of Small Thinking*, Bhaskar (2021) noted that some ideas can hold a lasting and outsized impact. And Google's ideas so far have had an indelible impact on business, society, and governments, including how people use the internet.

It is important to note that ideas do not come from thin air and that ideas morph, remix, and hold cross-objective uses (Bhaskar, 2021). Ideas, most importantly, possess histories. Those histories come sometimes for good and sometimes for ill.

Google's COVID-19 approach may become the gold standard of copying and pasting. Just hope Google did not copy the COVID-19 mitigation plan from the World Bank Group or Allied-Universal Security Services, because all the unvaccinated contractors would be terminated, even if they request religious exemptions.

Dr. Jonathan Reiner (as cited in Maxouris & Elassar, 2022) noted that anything learned at the onset of the COVID-19 pandemic is outdated, and "all these rules are out the window" (para. 15). The COVID-19 mitigation plan practiced by the United States government, state governments, and private industry are already outdated, and the continued practice of such flawed and outdated measures is detrimental to people. For example, Citigroup, the first Wall Street firm, announced it will terminate unvaccinated employees at the end of January, fully implementing its no-jab, no-job policy (Nguyen, 2022). With all that is known about COVID-

19 and its spread, including the vaccines, these types of policies have become idiotic.

Graham (2021) reported that a survey conducted noted that "only about one in 10 Americans say that receiving the Covid-19 vaccine would violate their religious beliefs, while about 60 percent say that too many people are using religion as an excuse to avoid vaccine mandates" (para. 1). This represents strong indicia that any American attempting to exercise his or her religious beliefs will certainly find either covert or overt hostility concerning vaccine mandates, if not find an outright denial altogether. Dershowitz (2021) would even accommodate the religious and medical exceptions, even though he would compel vaccines on everyone else medically able.

The same 60 percent of people have failed to understand that religious freedom forms a part of the basis of America's existence and why good men and women such as Martin King, Jr., Mahatma Gandhi, and Howard Thurman, to name a few, stood up to tyrannical backlash and physical assault.

When the lamp's light has become dim and hope seemed distant, Americans have always found solace in turning to their spiritual beliefs that are shrouded in an ethic of care. Religious beliefs have always been a moral compass, even though many have abused its message. In the words of Hamer (as cited in American RadioWorks, 1964) all "we want [is] to live as decent human beings, in America" (para. 37).

Some 22 months after the COVID-19 pandemic began, President Biden (as cited in the White House, 2021) said that the United States has "stockpiled enough gowns, masks, and ventilators to deal with the surge of hospitalizations among the unvaccinated" (Section, 6:18 – 6:25). President Biden's comments come one year and 10 days following the Food and Drug Administration's Emergency Use Authorization (EUA) for the use of the Pfizer COVID-19 vaccine. Such incendiary language comes from officials who should know better, federal, state, and local governments. Indeed, fear knows no limits. Unfortunately, these same government officials are talking to people who do not hold the skills to question the disseminated data nor do these people have access to the raw data to form their own views.

This is in a world where many Americans cannot identify Louisiana on a map and believe the United States and Mexico represent the most closely protected border in the world, a world where it has been noted that many Americans are not ready for a progressively global marketplace (Cable News Network (CNN), 2006). The theme of unprepared Americans is further echoed by J. Levy et al. (2012), who noted that educational failures leave Americans unable to compete and jeopardize the United States' capability to maintain a dominant worldwide economic footprint and sustain its leadership posture.

Copying and Pasting: The Appearance Factor

The appearance of doing something, anything is not science. These people, by now realize the vaccines are not sustainable and yet they are still terminating employees. Now, the terminations have reached the U.S. military. Liebermann (2021) 27 active Air Force service members were discharged following 37 that were in basic training. Over 200 Marines have been purged for refusal to take the COVID-19 vaccines (A. M. Miller & Tomlinson, 2021). This is part of the lip service that is paid to the men and women of the United States military.

In a turn of events for military members, however, United States District Court Judge Reed O'Connor wrote that "there is no COVID-19 exception to the First Amendment. There is no military exclusion from our Constitution" (*U.S. Navy Seals 1-26, et al. v. Joseph R. Biden, Jr., et al. No. 4:21-cv-01236-O*, 2022, p. 2). Albeck-Ripka (2022) reported that thousands applied for religious exemptions, not one of those request were granted.

Failure to recognize religious exemptions is a part of a larger assault on the Constitution, but more specifically religious rights. This assault on religious rights not only comes from those in charge of protecting our rights but also from private actors such as corporations and special interest groups.

Legitimate Copying and Pasting

People stand to gain from deliberately copying the successful strategies... —Katy Milkman

Copying and pasting are appropriate measures at times (Milkman & Duckworth, 2021). However, we must still be mindful of our uniqueness. And not just our uniqueness, but others' uniqueness too (Arnold et al., 2020).

Trout (2015) noted that "if you ignore your uniqueness and try to be everything for everybody, you quickly undermine what makes you different" (p. 15). What happens when an organization loses its difference, the company's burial plot awaits them at the brand graveyard.

The Problem of Copying and Pasting for Organizations

Anyone who has made a decision is usually extremely reluctant to change it, even in the face of overwhelming evidence that it is wrong. — Stuart Sutherland

I'VE BEEN IMITATED SO WELL, I'VE HEARD PEOPLE COPY MY MISTAKES. —JIMI HENDRIX

Copying and pasting underscore several problems for organizations: (a) organizations risk copying something wrong and (b) when copying something wrong, it wastes organizational resources and dismantles goodwill. Accordingly, organizations can find themselves overseeing myopic risk appraisals, concentrating only on short-sided interests while neglecting profound examples from past events and overlooking long-term risks (S. Taylor, 2021).

Copying Inequalities

You separate people into groups and make them hate one another so you can run them all. —Trevor Noah

Organizations are copying and pasting inequalities. Like governments that allow inequalities, corporations have also developed "a range of contradictory discourses and ideologies for the purpose of legitimizing the inequalities that already exist or that people believe should exist" (Piketty, 2020). So, talking about inequalities to these corporations and governments represents a futile exercise because they already have talking points to contradict anything to the contrary.

In the era of COVID-19, organizations have corporified inequalities. Bad jobs. Discouraged workers. Class. Poverty. Gender. Rank. Health care. Homelessness. Intergenerational income mobility.

The COVID-19 pandemic has exacerbated inequities in the workplace, and organizations compound such problems with mass termination policies which increase the myriad of employee, legal, and public relations questions (Ratcliffe & Wilson, 2021).

Copying Biases and Prejudice

There are no desperate situations, there are
only desperate people. —Heinz Guderian

Beyond the inequalities, organizations are also copying biases such as affinity bias. That is, organizations develop a predisposition for the vaccinated rather than the unvaccinated. Corporations are also copying prejudice. Prejudice results from flawed generalities and hostility that form a person's opinion (Allport et al., 1979).

There are unvaccinated chameleons in the room, in hospitals, in boardrooms, and all around us.

Before digging into the unvaccinated chameleons, it is also important to note that there are people at the other end of the spectrum, the over-vaccinated or the unauthorized vaccinated, those who were vaccinated before the United States government authorized doses for their age group and those obtaining fourth or fifth doses of COVID-19 vaccine, fraudulently (Chen, 2021; Morris, 2022). And then, there are the ones that breached other company COVID-19 rules such as Antonio Horta-Osorio, the former chairman of Credit Suisse, who resigned from the banking giant in disgrace (British Broadcasting Corporation (BBC), 2022b).

Qualtrics (2021) noted that about "30% of unvaccinated workers would consider misrepresenting their vaccination status or fabricating documents for a variety of reasons including keeping their jobs, eating out, flying on an airplane, going to the gym and more" (para. 1). Some employees have gone through great lengths to hide, shield, or escape termination, including lying about their vaccination status (Place, 2021).

Even though organizations understand biases are littered with cognitively loaded perceptual distortions, they marched through their organization disseminating terminations to the unvaccinated.

Bogus COVID-19 vaccine cards are being sold online (Diaz, 2021). Not just online, but also in person, COVID vaccination cards are being peddled everywhere. According to Kallingal and Boyette (2021) Tammy McDonald, a nurse out of Columbia, South Carolina, was charged with making phony COVID-19 cards. This included filling out individuals' biographical data and recording known lot numbers for vaccines yet to be administered (Kallingal & Boyette, 2021). Bogus COVID-19 cards are as real as it gets. The unsuspecting receiver of a COVID-19 card of this nature would never be able to suspect the cards were frauds.

In another high-profile account bogus COVID-19 vaccination cards, Cartaya and Elamroussi (2021) reported that Chief T. J. Smith of the Oakboro Police Department in North Carolina was alleged to have informed his police officers where they could obtain phony COVID-19 vaccination cards. Chief Smith was placed on administrative leave until the details of the incident are sorted out.

Another high-profile example of a fake COVID-19 vaccination card use is associated with the Buccaneers' Antonio Brown (Stroud, 2021). Based on the information presented by Stroud (2021), Antonio Brown, his girlfriend, and others engaged in a federal conspiracy to obtain a COVID-19 vaccination card. Yet, it appears that Antonio Brown and others will not be criminally sanctioned. Bumbaca (2021) reported that Antonio Brown will return to the Buccaneers after a three-week absence for faking the COVID-19 vaccination card.

Ashford (2021) reported that dozens of New York City employees were suspended without pay following an inquiry into the usage of bogus Covid-19 vaccine cards. Fake COVID-19 vaccine cards are not limited to New York. Bogus COVID-19 vaccination cards have found their way into every state in the country, including Washington, D.C. In response, for example, the District of Columbia Department of Insurance - Securities & Banking (2021) put out a general bulletin about the use of fraudulent COVID-19 vaccination cards.

Bergal (2021) noted that the black market is wide open. Where normally black market dealers would only interact with another black-market seller, the floodgates are open to all who desire phony COVID-19 vaccine cards (Bergal, 2021).

This is an American problem, created, of course, by America's elite and corporations. Society has placed people into categories (i.e., the vaccinated and the unvaccinated) which are littered with attitudes and emotions that may sway a corporation's response (Eberhardt, 2019). As P. Fuller et al. (2020) noted, until negative unconscious bias is rooted out of organizations, this will always limit the rise of greatness in an organization. Maxwell (2007) called this "the law of the lid" (p. 1) whereby the effectiveness of an organization is limited by its ability, which in this instance, is unconscious bias, the vaccinated and the unvaccinated.

With the negative outcomes of copying of biases and inequalities, copying and pasting other organizations' responses to the pandemic should be studied, not necessarily copied.

Chapter 3

Ineffectual Leadership Strategies

...because inadequate leaders did not know
what else to do. Such leaders knew, that they
could depend on fear, suspicion, hatred, need,
and greed... —Octavia E. Butler

On May 8, 1945, World War II was declared complete, although capitulation occurred twice, on May 7 and May 9, 1945 (Jähner, 2022; National WWII Museum, 1970). Yet today, two WWII bombs exploded, some 76 years, 6 months, and 23 days after WWII was declared over (Reuters, 2021). In another incident, according to McGreevy (2021), a residential construction project led to the discovery of an unexploded WWII ordnance, triggering area police to require locals, some 2,600 homes, to evacuate. Again, a WWII-era bomb exploded in 2020 with no human injury from the explosion (Reuters, 2020).

With COVID-19 becoming endemic, the point is clear: ineffectual and unfocused approaches (government or private sector) will have long and hard consequences for future generations and the global economies. If a comprehensive action plan is not developed and followed through, society will continue to experience disruptive explosions from COVID-19 like the WWII bombs exploding 76 years later. Collinson (2021) noted that the Biden administration has signaled an endemic shift to their approach. I am unsure of how well Biden's endemic strategy will be, especially considering other lackluster approaches by the government. One thing is clear, whatever approach is postured, many Americans, especially the terminated, unvaccinated will be left without the prospect of work in many regions of the country.

At the heart of organizations, even governments, copying and pasting represents a lack of an effective return-to-work strategy. Deloitte (2021) noted that strategy is key to a successful return-to-work policy.

With as much copying and pasting that has occurred, these corporate boards should be asking for what they are paying these CEOs? Day and Schoemaker (2019) noted that boards do not want to hear their leaders missed the boat; they expect action, competence, diligence, and results.

It is crunch time, and all these CEOs are organizing around an inorganic play that may not produce the organizational fit these corporations seek.

There are several ways to approach strategy but first, a company needs to develop a strategic management model.

Most of the copying and pasting that has recently occurred is a result of poor communication and lack of vision, not only in the C-suite, but with Joe, the plumber, Jane, the cashier, and John, the security professional. As a rule, poor communication can make a situation worse (Fink, 2013), which drives the importance of a discussion at all levels of an organization to connect strategy.

Developing Strategy

When you are angry, take no action. When you are fearful, know you are going to exaggerate the dangers you face. War demands the utmost in realism, seeing things as they are. The more you can limit or compensate for your emotional response, the closer you will come to this ideal. —Robert Greene

According to Gamble et al. (2018), a strategy requires organizations to put forth distinctive approaches that set them apart in their customers' minds.

Most of the CEOs seem to have forgotten that employees are their internal customers. So, it is not a stretch to believe these former internal customers are thinking, "what the F... k?" And if your organizations are still reluctant to treat employees like customers, MacArthur (2019) noted that forces within the market will "turn the idea of considering employees first into a have-to-have rather than a nice-to-have for employers" (para. 3).

Data from the Great Resignation bears out MacArthur's (2019) position about how to treat employees. Pre-pandemic, organizations treated employees as a nice-to-have rather than a have-to-have, opposite of MacArthur's suggestion. This allowed employers free reign. The free reign employers enjoyed allowed them to compromise employees, creating unhealthy toxicity within the workplace. According to Sull et al. (2022), "a toxic corporate culture is by far the strongest predictor of industry-adjusted attrition," and this quick attrition is influencing both blue- and white-collar jobs with equal force (para. 13).

It can be no clearer than this: Happier employees (internal customers) are associated with the organization-wide ability to deliver on a corporation's goals of external customer satisfaction (Chamberlain & Zhao, 2019). When these organizations decided to terminate unvaccinated employees, it created an extremely toxic culture, leaving a slew of employees holding the bag. Hence, *the mass termination of the unvaccinated employees, while leaving the remaining employees to hold the bag, created the ultimate middle finger for the outstanding employees.*

Clawson (1986) noted that people pick how they respond to the world around them. In their book, *Great by Choice: Uncertainty, Chaos, and Luck—Why Some Thrive Despite Them All*, Collins and Hansen (2011) said that "by preparing ahead of time, building reserves, maintaining 'irrationally' large margins of safety, bounding their risk, and honing their disciplines in good times and bad, they handle disruption from a position of strength and flexibility" (p. 112).

Day and Schoemaker (2019) noted that turbulence can be managed. And following Clawson (1986) that people select how they respond, these organizations choose to manage their turbulence in the manner and method to which people are less important to their overall goals.

CEOs forgot to develop people strategies. And when disruptive or lean moments come, the first tool sought to address the issue may not be the most effective such as mass termination. Considering Collins and Hansen's (2011) response to the disruptive nature of COVID-19, CEOs have no reserves built up and operate from a position of weakness and inflexibility, even after two decades with training wheels.

COVID-19, Omissions, and the Trolley

There is more politics in medicine than there is in politics. —Thomas E. Levy

It is easy to fall into an omission bias (i.e., the propensity to believe destructive actions as harsher than destructive inactions), particularly in an emergency or what has been styled as an emergency. Omission bias can lure people to stop thinking and to just act (Scarry, 2012; Spranca et al., 1991). Accordingly, society should not be enticed into going with the flow of everything told to them by corporations or governments, even in a pandemic (i.e., emergency) (Scarry, 2012).

The downside to acting without thinking can manifest in mediocre analysis, drive flawed perceptions, and enable other negative behaviors such as overgeneralization. Mass termination is an example of omission bias. Mass termination was an erroneous "trolley problem" (Thomson, 1976, p. 206) driven by affinity bias (i.e., predisposition for the vaccinated rather than the unvaccinated) and omission bias.

As more COVID-19 variants come online (i.e., Delta, Omicron, and any others), more people will be hurt by current positions and policies. Organizations have copied and pasted so much; they have failed to realize there could be more trolleys on the track. With this dynamic, K. J. Brooks (2021) reported that Moderna's CEO Stéphane Bancel expects that current vaccine efficacy will result in a less effective option against the Omicron variant. Indeed, there are more trolleys on the tracks.

Get Your Feet Off the Desk

We're living in an age where people need to
talk. They don't communicate. —Queen Latifah

In his book, *You Can't Lead with Your Feet on the Desk*, E. Fuller (2011) noted that it is time managers and leaders broaden their perspectives while also making richer connections with their organization. You cannot make such connections only by looking at what the competition is doing, organizations must also pay attention to what they are doing.

The Role of CEOs

Some leaders treat adversity as a stepping-
stone, others as a tombstone. —John C. Maxwell

When weighing organizational risks against mass termination, questions must be asked, for example, what is the risk to reputation by following others' COVID-19 policies. Sitting back watching today's corporations approach risk management seems as though they acquired their risk management from a crackerjack box. In the C-suite, *pluralistic ignorance appears to be at an all-time high*. This type of group dynamic has dropped the collective and individual intelligence levels.

CEOs understand that whether we are in a pandemic or not, this is a "reputation economy" (Fertik & Thompson, 2015, p. 1). CEOs also know that as Origgi (2017) argued, "reputations spread uncontrollably, are echoed back and forth, and reproduced themselves in the voices of others" (p. vii). This makes their mass termination approach doubly baffling.

American employers are not novices at addressing economic tumult. This makes the mass terminations more troublesome. Americans have seen their share of economic and postbellum transitions since World War II (Van Horn, 2014), so these corporate practices appear malfeasant at best, Bernie Madoff-like at worst, just criminal.

In his book, *A CEO Only Does Three Things: Finding Your Focus in the C-Suite*, T. Taylor (2020) argued that CEOs are responsible for three things: (a) culture, (b) people, and (c) numbers. CEOs hold ultimate authority over corporations and construct the most significant determinations about such corporations (Nohria & Khurana, 2010).

COVID-19 has exposed these corporations' backside, which appears to be only focusing on the numbers, disregarding the culture and the people. Former U.S. Secretary of State Rice (2011) noted that a "budget is the statement of priorities, not just a collection of numbers" (p. 341). In this COVID-19 pandemic, organizations communicated their priorities. This arouses the question, what type of organization do you desire to be known as?

Chapter 4

The Humanity of Policies and Procedures

It just never dawned upon them that I could understand, that I wasn't a pet, but a human being. —Malcolm X

Certainly, there is nothing wrong with creating policies and procedures. Creating ill-advised or ineffectual policies is where the problems come from. The ill-advised or ineffectual policies are where organizations lose face and add costs. For example, while many organizations have implemented COVID-19 vaccine mandates some hospitals and other organizations have begun to see their errors of their way, and thus have begun rolling back vaccine mandates from their employees (Cheng, 2021; Chuck, 2021; Whelan & Evans, 2021). Companies such as Amtrak, General Electric, and now Boeing have decided to roll back their vaccination requirements for employees. The same organizations now have a credibility issue.

Rudolph and Zacher (2021) noted that policies, especially during the COVID-19 pandemic, must be designed and facilitated to support employees. Thus, creating policies and procedures that lack an iota of basic humanity and the forceful rigidity to which such policies have been implemented, especially resulting in life-altering decisions based on relatively raw data, comes over as highly suspect. de Waal (2021) noted that in the beginning stages of a pandemic, often doctors and epidemiologists will be incorrect and convey ambiguous information. This erroneous and unclear guidance often arrives with the best of intentions. But there are exceptions to some of these doctors' objectives.

Policies that result from decision traps almost always result in false dichotomies (Hougaard & Carter, 2021; Russo & Schoemaker, 1989). *And when decisions are made from a narrow perspective, leaders trap themselves into a binary choice minefield where their abilities, character, and skills can be challenged.*

When leaders become trapped in a dichotomy of a binary choice minefield, it leaves no room for compassion, empathy, or all the things that make employees human. Compassion and empathy are important tools for an organization's leadership (Hougaard et al., 2021). When a person gets into a fight or flight mood of thinking, generally all that is thought about at that moment is survival. Because most leaders need to be trained in crisis leadership, the average leader's response becomes impotent, it is not firing on all cylinders.

In today's COVID-19 world, the same people heralded as heroes yesterday are scapegoats today (Weisman, 2021): the police officers, the nurses, the sanitation workers, the engineers, you know, "*the help.*" The help has "faced orchestrated gaslighting, marginalization, and scapegoating" (Kennedy, 2021, p. 24). Allport et al. (1979) noted that while society has advanced in so many positive ways, we still operate primitively when it comes to human relationships.

In today's COVID-19 world, compassion and wisdom are needed more than ever (Hougaard et al., 2020). As noted by the Dalai Lama (2009), "if you want others to be happy practice compassion; and if you want yourself to be happy practice compassion" ("Preface to the 10th Anniversary Edition," para. 2).

Practicing compassion means, for example, policies should not be designed to solely shift the burden from organizations to employees (Rudolph & Zacher, 2021). Indeed, implementing wholesale, burden-shifting, organizational policies always generates a goal congruence issue for an organization's control function.

The Right to Work

According to Wood (2016) "the bulk of society's work is done by propertyless labourers who are obliged to sell their labour-power in exchange for a wage in order to gain access to the means of life and of labour itself" (p. 7). Wood observed three disadvantages: (a) one is often propertyless, (b) one sells required labor power in the workforce to gain the means of life, and (c) one enters the market to gain access to the labor market itself.

Just Fighting

There is a unique hostility in these times. —
John R. Lewis

At the beginning of the COVID-19 pandemic, no one would have ever thought that they would not only have to fight for their lives from a biological agent but also an organizational system that is stacked against them. Fighting for unemployment benefits. Fighting to maintain proper housing. Fighting to feed yourself and your family. Fighting to keep the utilities on. Fighting to keep one's sanity. Fighting to maintain normalcy. And ultimately, you get so tired, you just fight. You are fighting on airplanes. You are fighting in restaurants. You are fighting at gas stations, just fighting. Hence, in the article, *America is Falling Apart at the Seams*, D. Brooks (2022) noted that "as Americans' hostility toward one another seems to be growing, their care for one another seems to be falling" (para. 10).

Undesirably, the fighting represents a part of what Poussaint (as cited in Ghaemi, 2011) noted that Martin King, Jr. fought diligently against, which is the "social economic desperation" (p. 103). The COVID-19 pandemic represents, in King's (as cited in Carson, 2001) words, "*a time when men [and women] experiencing in all realms of life disruption and conflict, self-destruction, and meaningless despair and anxiety*" (p. 45).

Employees have been drawn into social-economic desperation. Awkwardly, the desperation is flashing on televisions and social media, nationally and internationally. For example, the U.S. Department of Transportation - Federal Aviation Administration (2022a) data shows that in 2021, there were 5,981 unruly-passenger incidents. With the new year just beginning and by January 11, 2022, 76 unruly-passenger incidents were reported (U.S. Department of Transportation - Federal Aviation Administration, 2022b). In 2020, the Federal Aviation Administration (FAA) initiated 183 unruly-passenger investigations, but by the end of 2021, the FAA had begun 1075 unruly-passenger investigations. Accordingly, the stress of the pandemic is certainly impacting people's behavior.

Awkwardly, the world has been thrust into what Karpman (1968) styled as a "drama triangle" (p. 40). The significance of a drama triangle is that roles can switch but in switching roles, the most skilled change roles (immediately), according to Karpman (2007), to prevent transparency, and in doing so, they make everything a competition, repudiate everything and place everyone else on the defensive about everything. And if you ever ask him or her a question, you cannot nail him or her down on anything.

Chapter 5

The Aaron Rodgers Dilemma

*In a civilized world even bigots have a voice,
but in a bigoted world, the only place where you
can find reason and inclusion is prison. —Abhijit
Naskar*

Aaron Rodgers, quarterback of the Green Bay Packers, according to Morse (2021), Rodgers would not be participating in the football game against the Green Bay Packers and the Kansas City Chiefs, because of Covid-19 rules. At the time, Rodgers (as cited in Morse, 2021) described the experience as being 'in the crosshairs of the woke mob right now' (para. 3).

Whether it comes through admissions or not, any decent warm-blooded homo sapiens knows Rodgers is being shafted, shammed, and shunned. *It is the cancel culture, repackaged.* It is a gross cancel culture nipping away not only careers but also one's right to work.

After being featured in State Farm's commercial ads, for example, for approximately 10 years, Rodgers' ads are systematically disappearing (Valinsky, 2021). *We are witnessing a modern, Roman holiday and the television screen represents the chariots.* Aaron Rodgers is being publicly ostracized. Unfortunately, these organizations are making being unvaccinated psychologically uncomfortable through pressure campaigns and public floggings.

Arron Rodgers is a public figure, so that affords him a certain level of protection. The less fortunate include the blue-collar employees such as the Allied-Universal Security Services employees, the Walmart cashiers and stock clerks, etc., the lesser-known examples. The less fortunate employees have received the brunt of these unilateral decisions that deny their basic civil and human rights, the ability to make choices about their bodies.

Employees required better protections than what they had traditionally received, pre-COVID-19. There are sexual offender registries. There is a no-fly list. Yet, there are no corporate predator registries, replete with the callous acts that breach employees' well-being or safety.

Organizations are Showing their Backside

No respect. —Rodney Dangerfield

The downside to these mass terminations is now, such organizations have promulgated their official doctrine, but in doing so, others can now observe, according to Selznick and Simon (2011), the "subtleties unnoticed, ramifications ignored, and meanings crudely put" (p. 45). In other words, *everyone can smell the effluvium from your organization as the stench billows and the sludge builds*, not just current employees, but also future applicants and employees.

It is like wearing a hospital gown with an organization's backside showing because they fail to perform a rear-end analysis. This leads to the question: "Will the real Slim Shady please stand up?" (Eminem Music, 2010, section, 00:10).

The Assignment of Blame

Blame is just a lazy person's way of making sense of chaos. —Douglas Coupland

Stephens (2021) called on the end of assigning COVID-19 blame, noting, that the virus has made clowns of everyone who has cast blame about the pathogen as COVID-19 flipped directions, blanketing "blue states" when "red states" were being blamed, for example.

No one enjoys being blamed, especially when they were not at the root cause of it, whatever went wrong. Pearn and Mulrooney (2017) noted that all humans are prone to make mistakes, and more importantly humans understand how uncomfortable things can become when things do go wrong. It is humiliating, and when assignable mistakes are made, people, when they get blamed often just desire to stick their head in the sand.

Blame comes with an underbelly. And when it affects organizations, it can mutate into a blame culture, infecting the organizational culture and a corporation's employees.

Blame cultures arise from a set of attitudes that involve the abatement of risk tolerance (leading to the absence of risk-taking) or admitting to accountability (accepting that there were mistakes made) (Thomas et al.,

2018). A blame culture leads to employees always operating in a self-protection mode, and to protect themselves, they often choose to cast blame (Thomas et al., 2018).

Considering the larger stratum, COVID-19 exacerbates blame culture, leaving the unvaccinated to receive the harshest condemnation.

The unvaccinated were not responsible for COVID-19's development or its multiple mutations, yet still, unvaccinated employees became the reservoir for finger-pointing and vitriol. From the perspective of carriers, both vaccinated (Roberts, 2021; Tayag, 2021) and unvaccinated (Singanayagam et al., 2021; Vakil, 2021a) hosts have been responsible for communal transmission. Roberts (2021) said that "individuals who have had two vaccine doses can be just as infectious as those who have not been jabbed" (para. 1). COVID-19 has infected not only the unvaccinated but also the vaccinated and the boosted (Mandavilli, 2022c). For example, even with one of the highest vaccination rates in the world at 82%, Singapore has even experienced an elevated surge in COVID-19 (McCarthy, 2021).

Wuhan, China is the source of origin for coronavirus (COVID-19). According to Zimmer et al. (2021), patient X (i.e., the source of origin) was "a vendor in a large Wuhan animal market" (para. 1). Not only is Wuhan, China the source of the COVID-19 outbreak, but also the story told about bats does not hold water either, which according to Ridley (2020), "the simple story of an animal in a market infected by a bat that then infected several human beings no longer looks credible" (para. 1). In another blow-to-the-bat story, the University of Southampton (2021) was able to develop protein spikes consistent with the COVID-19 pathogen.

Today, however, the terminated, unvaccinated employees have received the assignment of blame. On balance, however, blaming the unvaccinated undermines the serious efforts of containing and solving the COVID-19 pandemic. Employers are off chasing red herrings, terminating hard-working employees, while COVID-19 is still circulating, even among the vaccinated.

Bacterium mutates, sometimes at random sequences and sometimes through the acquisition of other foreign bacteria (Zaman, 2020). Pathogens remain inert unless it is housed in a cell and it does not reproduce independently (Gilbert & Green, 2021). In other words, the mutation of COVID-19 does not rest upon the terminated, unvaccinated employees' contact with it, the mutation is a natural process. Bollinger and Ray (2021) noted that ribonucleic acid (RNA) type pathogens steadily adjust and progress.

Even when vaccinated, COVID-19 still circulates. "Vaccines are not 100% effective at preventing infection, [and] some people who are fully vaccinated will still get COVID-19" (U.S. Centers for Disease Control and Prevention (CDC), 2021b). Accordingly, the reason multiple vaccines exist is for redundancy (Gilbert & Green, 2021). Questions about the vaccine still abound. Some answers will be provided over time and some answers demand attention now.

A larger question that is not being asked is: How long are employees going to be forced to take the COVID-19 vaccines? And even more relevant, are employers going to force COVID-19 boosters? And if employers are going to force boosters, how many boosters do they think will be enough?

Anyone willing to critically think through the problems presented by the COVID-19 pandemic knows the current process was unrealistic from the beginning and it remains impractical. As was noted by Mandavilli (2022a), "trying to boost the entire population every few months is not realistic. Nor does it make much scientific sense" (para. 4).

On November 19, 2021, the U.S. Centers for Disease Control (CDC) recommended that all adults receive COVID-19 booster shots (Mandavilli, 2021). "Everyone ages 18 and older should get a booster shot either when they are 6 months after their initial Pfizer or Moderna series or 2 months after their initial J&J vaccine" (U.S. Centers for Disease Control and Prevention (CDC), 2021c, para. 1). Unfortunately, the World Health Organization Director-General Dr. Ghebreyesus (2021) disagreed with this approach, noting that "no country can boost its way out of the pandemic" (para. 29).

The CDC's booster endorsement follows what Syal (2021) noted about the fully vaccinated, which is "an increasing number of fully vaccinated people are being hospitalized or going to the emergency room" (para. 1). This information comes as the CDC noted that "mRNA COVID-19 vaccines... [i.e., Pfizer and Moderna] reduce the risk of infection by 91 percent for fully vaccinated people" (U.S. Centers for Disease Control and Prevention (CDC), 2021a, para. 1).

Tanner (as cited in ABC 4 Utah, 2021) noted that "we are not seeing proof that it is massively decreasing people from contracting or transmitting Covid" (section, 1:49 – 1:58). Although some protection is offered, COVID-19 infection remains possible (Bollinger & Ray, 2021).

The CDC has informed the public about a 91 percent reduction of risk for fully vaccinated people. At the same time, the World Health Organization (WHO) (2021b) has warned world leaders that "the presence of multiple mutations of the spike protein in the receptor-binding domain suggests that Omicron [variant] may have a high likelihood of immune escape from antibody-mediated protection [i.e., the vaccine-induced protection]" (page 5). In short, this means the fully vaccinated people may not be protected from the Omicron variant.

Kimball (2021a) reported on December 3, 2021, that the Omicron variant is in 38 countries. On January 2, 2022, omicron was reported everywhere at unprecedented levels (Maxouris & Yan, 2022). Now, we are left counting as the Omicron infects the world again. Omicron has brought higher transmissibility in its path (Kimball, 2021a). And the Omicron variant appears better able to escape vaccine-induced antibodies (Kimball, 2021b). Yong (2021) said it this way: "Boosting isn't a foolproof shield against Omicron" (para. 6). (Harlan, 2021) reported that data out of Denmark reveals that "people with two doses to be just as vulnerable to omicron infection as the unvaccinated" (para. 10).

Liu et al. (2021) noted that "a striking feature of this variant [Omicron] is the large number of spike mutations 31 that pose a threat to the efficacy of current COVID-19 vaccines and antibody therapies" (p. 2).

The CDC's endorsement of a COVID-19 booster comes 11 months 5 days after the initial COVID-19 vaccine was administered on December 14, 2020, in New York to Sandra Lindsay, an Intensive Care Unit nurse (Otterman, 2020). Lindsay just "happened to go first" after volunteering to get vaccinated (Tanner, 2021, para. 8). Lindsay received her second round on January 5, 2021, some 22 days later (Kovaleski, 2021).

Sandra Lindsay received the first shot after the first COVID-19 vaccine was authorized under the emergency use authorization on December 11, 2020, three days later (Otterman, 2020; U.S. Food and Drug Administration, 2021). Now Lindsay, according to Tanner (2021), has become a vaccination advocate.

On August 23, 2021, the emergency use authorization was lifted and the Pfizer-BioNTech COVID-19 Vaccine was approved with the blessing of the United States government (U.S. Food and Drug Administration, 2021). August 23, 2021, also marked another milestone, which included how American corporations would address vaccine requirements, which leads to the concern with boosters.

The reason boosters have become so prevalent is that vaccines are subject to the same rules of biology and chemistry as any other substance entering the biological stream. That is vaccines are subject to what is known as a half-life. A half-life represents the time necessary for a biological system, in this regard humans, to purge, through natural means, half of the amount of a substance, in this regard a COVID-19 vaccine, which has entered it. Hence, Lubell (2021) noted that immunity wanes with time.

Chapter 6

Psychologically Healthy Workplaces

Here's the news-flash: human beings
performing work in organizations are actually
different from mice running in mazes and
pressing bars for food pellets. —Pail L. Marciano

Van Hoof (as cited in Cohen, 2021) noted that if organizations were practicing and providing healthy workplaces before the COVID-19 pandemic, such traditions would ease unanticipated tensions brought on because of the pandemic.

The reverse is true too. Organizations not providing psychologically healthy workplaces can find it hard to convince employees their return-to-work policy considers them. Though it is not too late, organizations can begin proactive facilitation to support well-being in the workplace, giving organizations a handle on addressing the issues that would prevent a healthy, functional operation (Rudolph & Zacher, 2021).

According to Clark (2020), psychological safety occurs when employees feel that their (a) involvement is safe, (b) environment is conducive to learning safely, (c) participation is safe, (d) and challenges can be met without fear and reprisal. If an organization sabotages candor, prevents open disagreement, and turns away from the exchange of ideas, the possibility of you working in a psychologically unhealthy workplace is high (Edmondson, 2019). It is mind-numbing to work in a psychologically unhealthy environment. You desire to contribute ideas, but they are always knocked down. You see the organization about to make a mistake, but you do not say anything because it is unsafe to share.

The consequence of working in psychologically unhealthy workplaces results in the dissociating of employees' seeking system, which allows the innate instinct to create, discover, exchange meaning, and learn (Cable, 2019). And as such, employees become mindless automatons creating stagnation and starvation of ideas.

What are the Europeans doing?

We are more connected than ever with 'what' others are doing. But we are more disconnected than ever with 'how' others are doing. —Lysa TerKeurst

The Europeans are already providing a measure of psychologically healthy workplaces per their laws. According to the European Agency for Safety and Health at Work (2020), European employers must consider "both physical and psychosocial working environments" as part of their assessment ("Update your risk assessment," para. 1).

European employees also are involved in the risk assessments and analysis their companies must perform per EU law (European Agency for Safety and Health at Work, 2016). With the high levels of stress involved from the COVID-19 pandemic, the European guidance to employers is to approach all employees as though they are returning from an anxiety and depression leave (Cohen, 2021). These steps are part of the measures the EU required to control COVID-19.

Coe et al. (2021) noted that 1 out of 3 employees returning to work will have some form of a mental health problem such as anxiety or depression. Returning to work compounds the stress and trauma returning employees have already experienced because of COVID-19's second-order effects (Harfoush, 2021). Hudson (2021) noted that care, empathy, and understanding are imperative for a successful return to work.

The Permission to Disagree

Your boss is not your mother. —Debra Mandel

It is okay not to agree. What happens after disagreeing is where things go so wrong. According to M. Brown (2020), the three simple words, "I don't agree" rests at the heart of many conflicts. The conflict of going up against organizational groupthink (in-group and out-group). The pressure of standing alone. The prospect of being betrayed by their colleagues, friends, and family. And worst of all, the prospect of dealing with loss and grief alone after disagreeing with others. The humiliation. The uncertainty. The shame.

No one wants to be exposed to this type of social pressure, especially if such social pressure can at all be avoided. While many vaccinated employees may be masquerading about the office, that does not make them immune to the 'duck syndrome' (Gostick & Elton, 2021, p. 10).

Everyone has been exposed to unimaginable trauma from COVID-19's second-order effects. With the unvaccinated, terminated employees, however, this trauma is amplified. More than ever, this is the position *unvaccinated employees find themselves in, dealing with a social bomb. COVID-19 is a social bomb.*

Intergenerational Trauma

The answer may not lie within our own story as much as in the stories of our parents, grandparents, and even our great-grandparents. —Mark Wolynn

We are creating the next five generations of hurting people. Not everyone will be traumatized by the events of the COVID-19 pandemic. However, enough of the population will be left with an impression of the COVID-19 pandemic that it becomes a noticeable feature within society.

To overcome many of these issues, different sectors of business, government, and people must come together for a viable solution. According to (Brunnermeier, 2021), "a society is resilient if all, or at least most, individuals have the option to react in order to bounce back. In a non-resilient society, some people might never recover from a severe crisis" (p. 17).

Not everyone experiences traumatic events the same (L. Curran, 2019). Some may develop post-traumatic stress disorder while others may be resilient enough to develop posttraumatic growth (American Psychiatric Association, 2013; Maitlis, 2020; Tedeschi et al., 2020).

Take, for example, Eli (as cited in Epstein, 2019), a child of parents of the Holocaust, said that "being their child has given me a certain depth, a seriousness about life that most people can't possibly have" (p. 21).

Something was robbed from Eli's childhood. The "traumatic inheritance" can hold a profound impact on people through "historical trauma" (Hübl et al., 2020, p. xv). Most Americans have dealt with trauma by denial, though trauma does not fade away, even with contemporary psychological intervention, the trauma continues the assault through moral injury (Duran & Ivey, 2019).

The shock and awe from COVID-19's social effects will live on through intergenerational trauma, defined by a single thread, how society split apart rather than come together. This includes, how organizations were playing musical chairs, unprepared, with a social bomb like COVID-19, playing footsie with other corporations while their employees suffered.

Harsher still, and it will survive in the annals of history, is how corporations capitalized—just pounced on—the debility of the moment— the COVID-19 pandemic—terminating the most vulnerable of society. What organizations did in the COVID-19 pandemic gives new context and meaning to Churchill's (as cited in Mutter, 2016) immortal words: "Never let a good crisis go to waste" (para. 1).

Foster et al. (2021) said it this way:

The fearful were the perfect victims for those with cooler heads who recognised that this was a unique opportunity to seize power and wealth for themselves. The paralysis of the fearful led in the end to heartless neglect, social disintegration, widespread theft, and totalitarian control. (p. 7)

Chapter 7

What Perfect Controls?

The dangers have become much more subtle—
they come in the form of people (not leopards)
and their tricky psychology, and the delicate
political and social games we have to play. —
Robert Greene

Merchant (1982) noted that perfect controls do not exist. Yet these companies respond as though perfect controls exist. It is delusional. Taylor's (2009) own scientific management rejects what is going on today, but organizations have insisted on these rules of thumb over science.

Certainly, corporations should be familiar with upheaval and uncertainty, especially after the last 20-plus years (Hannah et al., 2021). However, companies, as Ivancevich (2010) noted, continue to habituate short-run steps, thinking only about present performance. Such habituated short-run steps (i.e., narrow framing) lie at the feet of market manipulation.

The Answer to Perfect Controls

The bullshitter ignores these demands
altogether. He [or she] does not reject the
authority of the truth, as the liar does, and
oppose himself [or herself] to it. He [or she] pays
no attention to it at all. By virtue of this, bullshit
is a greater enemy of the truth than lies are. —
Harry G. Frankfurt

Terminating employees because of their COVID-19 vaccination status results from thinking that perfect controls exist when the opposite is true. Deming and Cahill (2018) noted that "common causes and special causes" of variation do exist (p. 26), and blaming the unfortunate, in this case, the unvaccinated, does not change the fact there is a fundamental systems issue requiring correction.

Everything, worldwide, relies on people and systems (Kaufman, 2012; Kurtzman et al., 2004; Silbiger, 2012). Understanding the COVID-19 pandemic response requires an understanding of systems. Even an understanding of systems leaves information wanting because it is also important to recognize the statecraft at play. And to appreciate the statecraft is to realize the levers being pulled, according to Scott (2020), "to make a society legible, to arrange the population in a way that simplified the classic state functions of taxation, conscription, and prevention of rebellion" (p. 1). Ultimately, Scott (2020) noted that systems and a country's statecraft lead to a "workforce more legible—and hence manipulable—from above and from the center" (p. 2). In other words, systems and statecraft set people up to be controlled, even through things as simple as last names (the last name is a system).

However, there are basic and specific errors implicit in the operations of a system (Rutherford, 2019). Yet still, the terminated, unvaccinated employees have become the scapegoats of the COVID-19 pandemic. How unfortunate.

It is not the first time within a pandemic innocent people were blamed, for the Bubonic plague (i.e., the Black Death), for example, violence was carried out against blameless people (Harsh, 2020). Instead of overt violence against the unvaccinated, for instance, organizations simply selected to just terminate their unvaccinated population.

These are bad faith mass terminations, and these CEOs know it. When people make bad faith decisions, they sidestep responsibility by blaming others (Myers, 2005), in this instance, the unvaccinated.

Without perfect control, and believe me, these CEOs know that no perfect controls exist, and by terminating unvaccinated employees, such terminations are done in bad faith. Bad faith because CEOs know no such thing as perfect control exists. In truth, the problem with terminating employees because of their vaccination status leaves society no better off today than yesterday, especially by making such hasty, knee-jerk decisions.

Chapter 8

Mass Terminations, COVID-19, and HIPAA

Being cut off... at a time when you feel most
vulnerable... leaves you feeling cornered and
desperate. —Virginia Eubanks

Corporations, in record number, have terminated employees because either such employees did not disclose their COVID-19 vaccination status or declined to get vaccinated.

Normally, companies cannot obtain employees' medical records under the Health Insurance Portability and Accountability Act of 1996 (HIPAA) (Office for Civil Rights (OCR) - U.S. Department of Health & Human Services, 2020), so they coerce employees' self-disclosure through a pressurized environment (Hanna & Holcombe, 2021) and terminate employees for failure to comply (A. Smith & Nagele-Piazza, 2021).

The Intolerable Workplace

It's either I'm working, thinking about
working, just finishing working or feeling guilty
about not working. Need balance. —Anonymous

An intolerable workplace has become an understatement in the era of COVID-19. Amplified by the discrimination, indifference, and pretentious spectacle, in the era of the COVID-19 workplace, as the great ills of organizations occur, looking in the opposite direction has become commonplace.

The pressure is so thick, organizations openly coerce employees and their families. Talk about a pressure campaign, some organizations are even jacking up employees' families' insurance rates for those who remain unvaccinated against COVID-19 (WAFB Staff, 2021). According to Vakil (2021b) noted that Nevada state employees and their adult dependents will be hit with a monthly surcharge for eluding vaccination.

The Mother of All Carrots and Sticks

*Work provides an 'artificial' world of things,
distinctly different from all natural
surroundings. —Hannah Arendt*

Andrews (2021) reported that being unvaccinated could "follow workers beyond the grave" as organizations have begun to decline death benefits (para. 1). This is a surreal moment. Just bizarre. Imagine working for an organization all your natural life, and not only do they slap you from the grave, but the company saps your death benefit by not honoring the insurance policy to which you have paid, simply because one has selected not to be vaccinated.

Companies own the master insurance policy to which employees buy into, so they control the insurance policy. Talk about insanity, organizations have run wild in the COVID-19 environment. Owning the master insurance policy provides organizations with a broad swath of legal rights. Setting the terms and conditions is just one right an organization holds by owning the master insurance policy.

Remote Terminations

*Evil no longer exists in contrast to good;
rather, there is a new inhumanity:
indifference—that is to say, complete alienation,
complete indifference vis-à-vis life. —Erich
Fromm*

Employers are terminating employees remotely (Simons, 2020). Remote termination has become a tool of the COVID-19 pandemic. In one of the largest mass terminations of the COVID-19 pandemic, Fieldstadt et al. (2021) reported that 900 Better.com employees were terminated via Zoom video conference call. Vishal Garg, CEO of Better.com, accused 250 of the 900 of stealing time, clocking in for eight hours a day, but only working for two hours (Towey, 2021).

While the COVID-19 pandemic has highlighted McDonaldization and how technology has sped things up, this only adds to the evidence that employees have been devalued.

The Forbes Human Resources Council (2018) offered 11 practices to allow employees to be terminated gracefully. Of the 11 termination approaches, four practices are instructive here, which include:

- demonstrating respect,
- remembering employees are people,
- separating the personal, and
- surprising employees are inappropriate.

The terminated, unvaccinated employees have not been treated with the respect they deserve. The terminated, unvaccinated employees have not been treated like people. The terminated, unvaccinated employees were surprised with termination, leaving them baffled. And lastly, we are people, and this is personal. Did those employees work all those hours because they wanted to? Did those employees miss opportunities to be with their families because they wanted to?

Regrettably, this is how organizations can stand there in a less dignified manner, offer terminated employees an option, according to one employer's representative "to re-apply for their positions should they decide to get vaccinated against COVID-19 and wish to return" (Keith, 2021, para. 3). Accordingly, *the shameless have no bottom to which they will sink.*

Terminated for Misconduct

Make the endings a normal occurrence and a normal part of business and life, instead of seeing it as a problem. —Henry Cloud

EVERY MAN HAS THE RIGHT TO LIFE, TO BODILY INTEGRITY. — POPE JOHN XXIII

Employers are using their policies and procedures as hatchets to deny unvaccinated, terminated employees unemployment benefits because the unvaccinated was terminated for "misconduct for not following company policy" (A. Smith, 2021, para. 15). Misconduct means an employee has been terminated for cause in many states (Rowan, 2021).

Unfortunately, this issue raises a larger question about one's bodily integrity and privacy rights. As a human being, one has rights over his or her bodily integrity in two aspects: the external and the internal. That is, one's rights extend to anything on the body and in the body. History is instructive here as there was one regime that held one's body was considered the property of the community (S. R. C. Hicks, 2010).

The Common Good and Community

Treating other people as if they were objects is one of the worst things you can do to another human being, to ignore their subjectivity, their thoughts and feelings. —Dimon Baron-Cohen

Vermeule (as cited in Goldberg, 2021) championed vaccine mandates and wrote that "even our physical liberties are rightly ordered to the common good of the community when necessary" (para. 3). No good can be had from the ordered surrender of liberty to a community.

As Becker and Keen (2007) noted, "the root of humanly caused evil is not man's animal nature, not territorial aggression, or innate selfishness, but our need to gain self-esteem, deny our mortality, and achieve a heroic self-image" ("Forward," para. 13).

It is in these types of analogs that become so destructive to individual liberty. Advocating vaccine mandates for the common good sounds like talking points directly from Adolf Hitler himself if he were alive. It is important to note that, during Hitler's rule, it was not uncommon to be confronted with "outlandish assertions from seemingly educated and intelligent persons" (Shirer, 2011, p. 355). And the same is true today.

Advocates of the common good would deny people a right to choose for themselves what is best for themselves, and their families. Then, they go stand up in front of the United States Supreme Court talking about their rights to choose but are willing to deny my rights to choose. What hypocrites.

Being terminated for misconduct holds all sorts of ethical implications for one's bodily integrity while in the employment of another. Accordingly, privacy rights are just the beginning.

Privacy Rights

"All human beings have three lives: public, private, and secret." —Gabriel García Márquez

In conducting mass terminations, companies rely on government regulation that violates employees' privacy rights.

Employers use the United States Supreme Court case *Jacobson v. Massachusetts, 197 U.S. 11* (1905). There are reasons context matters. And when dealing with employees' rights, context is king. The court did rule that exact way, this is being argued by people who use that argument. But here is the context:

- women had no voting rights,
- the Supreme Court had not taken up a case on privacy rights,
- Jim Crow was rampant, and
- *The Adventures of Huckleberry Finn* and *The Adventures of Tom Sawyer* were banned in many libraries.

Today, if libraries were to ban The Adventures of Huckleberry Finn or The Adventures of Tom Sawyer, it would be a national scandal. Yet today, many people have given up on their right to liberty.

Here is more context: Even with smallpox infusing its ravaging effect on society at the time, neither the Massachusetts court nor the United States Supreme Court violated Mr. Jacobson's bodily autonomy, but simply leveraged a $5.00 fine (Heckenlively, 2021). Being fined a $5.00 fine is much different from being terminated from one's employment. The question then comes to mind: Was a person's life more important in 1905 or now? We can see how far people have evolved in their concern about human rights by assessing this issue. Have we thrown liberty out the door?

Here is what an interdisciplinary group of attorneys and other professionals had to say about coercive practices concerning health policy:

One practical reason for protecting constitutional rights is that it encourages social solidarity. People are more likely to trust officials who protect their personal liberty. Without trust, public officials will not be able to persuade the public to take even the most reasonable precautions during an emergency, which will make a bad situation even worse.

The public will support reasonable public health interventions if they trust public health officials to make sensible recommendations that are based on science and where the public is treated as part of the solution instead of the problem. Public health programs that are based on force are a relic of the 19th century; 21st-century public health depends on good science, good communication, and trust in public health officials to tell the truth. In each of these spheres, constitutional rights are the ally rather than the enemy of public health. Preserving the public's health in the 21st century requires preserving respect for personal liberty. (Mariner et al., 2005, p. 588)

In the case of *Griswold v. Connecticut, 381 U.S. 479* (1965), the U.S. Supreme Court held: "A right to privacy can be inferred from several amendments in the Bill of Rights" (the Holding). The right to privacy is a right enshrined in the U.S. Constitution that was first recognized through Justice Louis Brandeis' iconic dissent in *Olmstead v. United States, 277 U.S. 438* (1928), in which he laid down the framework for privacy and noted that the U.S. Constitution protects individuals "in their beliefs, their thoughts, their emotions and their sensations" (p. 277).

Here is the problem with having privacy rights no one respects: With issues prompted by COVID-19 moving at such a rapid pace, the multithreaded damage will have already taken place without a remedy at law. To wait 37-plus years for the Supreme Court to hash out the details, if at all, is by far injustice itself. Until that time, *privacy rights have become a disfavored right*, a close second behind gun rights.

Chapter 9

Stalinist-Style Deportations

"Ideas are not intellectuals' toys: ideas have consequences, for good and for ill, in what even intellectuals sometimes call 'the real world'"
—George Weigel

While we live in the United States, the COVID-19 practices feel eerily similar to Stalin's totalitarian control, which also similarly denied citizens their inalienable rights (Ryzhkov, 2011). Stalin is often described as a man barren in compassion, obstinate and unyielding. Lacking compassion, obstinate, and unyielding behavior has been documented and witnessed from many of the organizations that have elected to implement COVID-19 mandates. And like Stalin, *COVID-19 terminations moved unvaccinated employees out of the workplace like Stalinist-style deportations, simply because of personal distrust and insecurity of the unvaccinated* (i.e., representativeness heuristic).

For the unvaccinated, getting labeled comes with a stigma. Fletcher (as cited in Balch, 2021) noted that "the overemphasis on fear and disincentives can lead to stigma, marginalizing populations that are already marginalized" ("Potential for equity issues," para. 2).

Stigma for the unvaccinated, in its basic form, according to (Goffman, 2009), means reducing an employee from his or her "whole and usual person to a tainted, discounted one" (p. 2). The reduction of wholeness came the moment the notice was given: get vaccinated or else. *The or else has included a slew of negative reactions heaped upon the unvaccinated. It was like the unvaccinated emanate a stench like approaching a large cattle farm. You just know, you are going to smell cow dung.*

Penick (as cited in ABC 4 Utah, 2021) said that "there is not just one answer [get vaccinated or else]. 'You must have a vaccine.' That's just not... That's just not American!" (section, 2:05 – 2:12).

The unvaccinated have been labeled as socially deviant. Wolpe (2013) observed that once categorized as socially deviant by society, a person feels deviant regardless of the existence of a definition. When a person or group is labeled as socially deviant, history is indicative of the pains and penalties imposed on the socially deviant including mass extermination.

As a young child, I learned that when people do not have respect for you, they will do anything to you. As I grew up, I have watched the expression of disrespect play out in multiple channels of my life, especially in the workplace. So, I know how disrespect and stigma encroach into every facet of one's life without taking a stand.

Punishment by Other Means

In the article, *How to hold unvaccinated Americans accountable*, Dr. Altschuler (2022) named several methods to hold the unvaccinated answerable for merely expressing their constitutional rights. First, Dr. Altschuler would charge more for insurance. Second, Dr. Altschuler would give the vaccinated more incentives such as lower deductibles.

After many unvaccinated people have been punished through termination from their jobs, punishment by other means is a secondary punishment.

Just stick the screwdriver in the unvaccinated and turn it and keep turning it. This sums up Dr. Altschuler's (2022) views and others who posture the same ideas.

Unfortunately, the thing about prejudice is that, as Allport et al. (1979) noted, our lifestyles provide substance that fuels it, which can lead people to the "brink of prejudice" (p. 25). Accordingly, people that offer these masochistic thoughts about the unvaccinated will keep pushing such unbridled policies until such cannibalistic regulations show up at their door. Hence, a vaccine for their sadism is necessary.

Connected Influence

Reciprocation, liking, and unity for when relationship cultivation is primary... —Robert B. Cialdini

Some would argue, for instance, that no single person is pushing the buttons. For those contemplating such arguments, this minimizes how networks work and the power of multiplex relationships. Kadushin (2012) noted how network influence works which encompass four practices including:

(1) the same kinds of people come together; (2) people influence one another and in the process become alike; (3) people can end up in the same place; (4) and once they are in the same place, the very place influences them to become alike. (p. 20)

Ultimately, no single person needs to be in control, all that is needed is a disseminated idea, an ideology. In his book, *The Will to Be Human*, Arieti (1972) said, "if he [or she] controls your ideas he [or she] will soon control your actions, because every action is preceded by an idea" (p. 83).

Ideas when planted can sow some of the most unrelenting social decadence and destruction man has witnessed. Jung (1964), in discussing ideas, noted that

Just when people were congratulating themselves on having abolished all spooks [belief in demons], it turned out that instead of haunting the attic or old ruins the spooks [demons] were flitting about in the heads of apparently normal Europeans. Tyrannical, obsessive, intoxicating ideas and delusions were abroad everywhere, and people began to believe the most absurd things, just as the possessed do. (p. 212).

Individuals and social advancement are all subject to the influence of ideas. As such, it is critically imperative to guard against such influences by being informed, first through history and then through current events. Being informed allows a society to prevent the rampant insanity and mass psychosis that has occurred throughout the COVID-19 pandemic, worldwide. Jung (2014) warned about the infectious nature of ideas when put forth, and noted that when ideas are planted, even when others put forth well-meaning or reasonable responses, they will find themselves trying to survive the sharks, getting eaten alive.

Chapter 10

Life Measures Attached to Working

> *In the best of times 'security' has never been
> more than temporary and apparent. But it had
> been possible to make the insecurity of human
> life supportable by belief in unchanging things
> beyond the reach of calamity—in God, in man's
> immortal soul, and in the government of the
> universe by eternal laws of right. —Allen Watts*

Detert (2018) noted that jobs are appended to the vital allowances and protections of life: health care, retirement, social security, and well-being, to name a few. Attaching these life measures to the workplace is one of the greatest feats of capitalism.

The Largest Feat of Capitalist

> *The modern bourgeois society that has
> sprouted from the ruins of feudal society has not
> done away with class antagonisms. It has but
> established new classes, new conditions of
> oppression, new forms of struggle in place of the
> old ones. —Karl Marx*

Capitalism's reach extends deep into the mechanics of the American system. At the Social Security Administration, retirement is associated with work. According to the U.S. Social Security Administration (SSA) (2021), it takes an average of 10 years to even earn the credits needed to receive a social security retirement, which is contingent upon receiving four credits maximum per $1,470.00 a year. The truth is employees have been on their own. Every year, the amount increases (SSA, 2021).

Tomorrow's Skid Row

> *In bourgeois society, men are estranged, in
> specifiable ways, from the ties to society which*

alone confer their 'humanity' upon them. —
Anthony Giddens

If one does not earn enough social security credits, among other social safety nets, good luck, which, according to Obama (2008) "you're on your own" (para. 21). Unfortunately, terminating employees for their vaccination status today, without the ability to work, is building tomorrow's skid row.

One of the immediate issues for this new skid row is that most may believe that homelessness eliminates the bills "normal people" have. Elimination of bills and burdens for the homeless is the furthest thing from the truth. According to Yearwood (2021), aside from the trauma and pain of being homeless, it cost her $54,000 for one year of homelessness. Not only are the homeless saddled with debt, but also they are criminalized (Yearwood, 2021). This is the shock that awaits many people, including the terminated, unvaccinated employees from the corporate and public policies that have resulted from the COVID-19 pandemic.

In history, every time the majority has been this disruptive to a resident subgroup of society, they have been burned, burned at the stake, burned in ovens by the thousands, and now burned by corporate and public policies.

Without the ability to earn a living, such a draconian approach removes the terminated, unvaccinated employees' ability to function in society. *Talk about hunting, no. Cannot afford a hunting license. Talk about fishing, no. Cannot afford a fishing license. Talk about food, no. Cannot afford a meal.* The mass termination of Americans pushes the people you know well, the people you worked with into the fringes of society. Ultimately, the mass terminations are influencing the public policy of tomorrow and beyond.

Employees' Utility

The aim of life is self-development. To realize
one's nature perfectly, — that is what each of us
is here for. People are afraid of themselves,
nowadays. They have forgotten the highest of all

duties, the duty that one owes to one's self. —
Oscar Wilde

Affixing life measures to the workplace allows organizations to maintain a constant supply of stooges. Further, it allows organizations to hijack employees' utility unwittingly and maintain operant conditioning (i.e., carrots and sticks) at the employees' expense and destabilize their attached life measures (i.e., health care, retirement, social security, and well-being). The entire practice is antithetical to public policy and human rights.

The Golden Handcuffs

An elephant is in the room when something
obvious is going on and nobody talks about it,
and we pretend it's not there. —Mike Bechtle

According to Robinson (2014) "work has become a defense against relationships, and a balance has been lost" (p. 21). A little more here. A little more there. Eventually, one becomes bound, attached to the golden handcuffs, or at least there is a thought that such handcuffs are golden until one peeks into the misery of the workplace. Indeed, the working class certainly knows about what Barone (2004) styled as "hard America" ("Introduction," para. 5).

The Disconnected Mind and Body

Leave your brain at home because we'll think
for you. –Allied-Universal Security Services,
Manager

Hard America has certainly ensured employees engage in the toxic habit of not being mentally present where their feet are (O'Neil, 2021), stripping employees' joie de vivre, and ensuring employees are not present for the most important moments of life. This represents a part of the reason employees have a love-hate relationship with companies (Bank et al., 2017).

Chapter 11

Moving Backwards

*You can't go forward and backward at the
same time. —Steve Harvey*

As part of the chief macroeconomic objectives, a nation is tasked with three primary functions, which include seeking economic expansion, maximum employment, and price-level stability. In the COVID-19 era, mass terminations drive distortions in the labor market, depressing full employment. The result can lead to suboptimal performance and prolonged imbalance requiring more government mediation (Tuerck, 2021).

In his book, *Competitive Advantage of Nations*, Porter (2011) noted that "the principal economic goal of a nation is to produce a high and rising standard of living for its citizens" (p. 39). COVID-19 has struck at the very fabric of Porter's assertion, especially with organizations deploying mass terminations as a corporate approach. This is a *what the f... k* (WTF) moment! Worst of all, the second-order effects from COVID-19 will be felt for decades.

Breaking the Stride

*It took a lot of time to find my stride, and it
was really humbling. —Zuleikha Robinson*

What is worse about these COVID-19 mass termination objectives is they break the stride of the forward progress to which the world is moving. For example, the United Nations (UN) (2018) has implemented 17 Sustainable Development Goals (SDGs). Of the UN's (2018) 17 SDGs, mass terminations bear a negative influence on:

- goal 3 ("good health and well-being");
- goal 8 ("decent work and economic growth");
- goal 9 ("industry, innovation, and infrastructure"); and
- goal 10 ("reducing inequalities"). (00:00 - 01:10)

Cann (2015) noted that achieving goals three, eight, nine, and ten can be achieved. For example, Cann noted:

- that innovation and technology can provide a bridge to healthier living;
- that well-performing and transparent organizations can safeguard rights (in general), decrease overcomplication, and reduce exploitation;
- that collaborative innovation can open doors to resilient and trusted frameworks; and
- that using ethical values as levelers can stimulate solutions and drive policy.

Mass COVID-19 termination reduces and undermines the progress made on the SDGs to date. Even further, mass termination undermines the World Economic Forum's environment, social, and governance (ESG) framework. The World Economic Forum has put organizations on notice that human capital is important to its ESGs (Bremen et al., 2021).

Chapter 12

Deindividuation and Social Facilitation

We must learn that, despite their trademark lack of emotion, sociopaths are 'emotion-eaters.' They have an intense desire to witness their control over us by inciting our confusion, anger, and fear. They feed off the negative emotions of others. —Martha Stout

Mass terminations follow a very eerie path very seldom taken throughout human history. It is instructive to highlight history here because, this level of mass deindividuation (i.e., losing one's identity in a group) has had an infrequent appearance in human history.

Wholesale conformity and mass deindividuation, driven by social facilitation (i.e., the arousal baring presence of others), has not been witnessed since 1933. After the Nazis expanded their power base, book burnings began shortly afterward, but the initial book burnings were not directed by the Nazi regime, it was initiated and supervised by students (S. R. C. Hicks, 2010). In similar regard, mass terminations were not directed by the U.S. government, which means such terminations remain unendorsed practices facilitated by corporations. When the official state-sanction book burning began, the notion remained the same, smudging out ideas, not simply control over beliefs and bodies (Manning, 2014).

Yet another event from 1933 is also instructive here: The Great Depression. Nineteen thirty-three and the Great Depression was not an enjoyable time for organizations, employees (the select few employees with jobs), and the unemployed. Hence, Americans and the world knows what an uninhibited corporate practice can do to a fledgling economy, especially when a government fails to mediate its impact.

Modern examples of indiscriminate conformity, collective deindividuation, and social facilitation include the Ku Klux Klan burning crosses in African American residents' yards, the looting and burning of buildings in the riots of Atlanta (2020), Baltimore (2015), and Ferguson (2014). One thing that is clear from the examples presented—and none of it is good for society—is the social cost of correcting these social ills

71

that drove such dark behaviors. Here again, mass terminations are not good for society and the cost to correct such an injury is high.

Physical Anonymity

It [anonymity] brings out the worst in humans. —Jonathan Taplin

As organizations have cozied up with one another, their physical anonymity has been increased in the era of COVID-19. The increase of physical anonymity of corporations in the era of COVID-19 has allowed such organizations to do things to employees such as mass termination with the silent blessing of the government. Be forewarned. Beware of kissing the signet ring too soon. If anonymity brings out the worst in humans, what does it do to a juggernaut of corporations with money, power, and a will to use it (anonymity) indiscriminately?

Sustainability and Mass Termination

Stepping in shit is inevitable, so let's either see it as good luck, or figure out how to do it less often. —Matthew McConaughey

Looking at mass terminations from a sustainability perspective, the policies are even more grotesque. Stakeholders (i.e., in this circumstance, employees) enhance organizational sustainability (Peloza et al., 2012). But the corporate policy of mass termination decreases the terminated, unvaccinated employees' sustainability. For one, mass terminations decrease the terminated, unvaccinated employees' ability to provide for themselves and their families. And two, mass termination compounds COVID-19's negative impact while also altering a community.

It is common knowledge that early childhood trauma or adverse childhood experiences (ACEs) hold negative and long-term reactions over a child's mental health well into adulthood (Sullivan, 2019). Yet, organizations have terminated children's fathers, mothers, grandparents, and neighbors amid the COVID-19 pandemic. These terminations compound an already outsized problem for children, especially because the children are already observing the stress, for example, from their parents' experiences from the COVID-19 pandemic and generally the stress of daily life.

In the book, *Childhood, Interrupted: Raising Kids During a Pandemic*, Gupta (2021) noted that children's childhoods are being canceled whether it is realized or not through the missed social opportunities and rapid changes that have occurred, to name a few. As a result of this problem, according to Gupta (2021), children often act as a mirror instead of a sponge. This means that children will often replay or recast their experiences similarly. Therefore, these mass termination policies are not only destructive in the immediacy of today but also well into the future.

The Great Political Bandwagon is Coming

The rights of every man are diminished when the rights of one man are threatened. — John F. Kennedy

When the data begins mounting about the mass terminations, policymakers are going to get on the bandwagon too, but in the opposite direction from these corporations, especially when they *evaluate the compound devastation that has dampened their communities based upon the toll of such organizational practice.*

According to Bernanke (2015), "when a serious pandemic occurs, significant damage to the broader economy is almost inevitable" (p. 400). COVID-19, according to Zakaria (2020), has presented colossal economic, social, and political injury to which the damage has not been observed since World War II. Mass termination is a part of the considerable damage to the United States' economy and social order.

Eventually, the United States will address the discrimination from COVID-19 as per the International Covenant on Civil and Political Rights (ICCPR) standards, but Article 22 of the ICCPR does allow room for countries to address public health emergencies such as COVID-19 (United Nations, 1965).

History is indicative here because when the United States, the United Kingdom, the Soviet Union, and the Republic of China (i.e., the Big 4) met in Washington D.C. in 1944 and established the United Nations in 1945, they had no intention of honoring human rights. When the issue of human rights came up, the Big 4 did everything they could to derail even the mention of human rights (Lauren, 2013, Chapter Lecture 18).

Even today, these same countries talk about human rights with flowery language publicly but approach it in an antagonistic and contentious way when challenged.

For instance, the calls to increase social protection have already begun to mount (AFL-CIO et al., 2021). Social protection, according to AFL-CIO et al. (2021), embodies an integral part of the international labor framework, it represents an internationally established human right, and it constructs a part of the United Nations SDGs.

Part 2

Chapter 13

If It Doesn't Make Dollars, It Doesn't Make Sense

The devil is in the details—Anonymous

Behind these incognito, return-to-work policies manifest an illness. Gottlieb (2021) noted that COVID-19 had been circulating since at least January 2020. However, Markson (2021) pointed out that discussions were being had as early as November 22, 2019, in Washington, D.C., about a novel coronavirus in Wuhan, China, and how Chinese citizens were using chatrooms to discuss its effects.

Many events occurred on November 22, 2019, but there is none more salient than the closure of a Colorado school to thwart a virus epidemic, which later resulted in the shutting down of the entire school district (Padilla, 2019). Shutting down the Mesa County Valley School District foreshadows the closing of schools and businesses to come as COVID-19 spread its deadly effects across the United States.

It is important to remember, according to Springer Nature (2020), who proffered February 6, 2020, as the date of origin for the first COVID-19 death in the United States, that COVID-19 represents a worldwide event. Thirty-four days later, after the first death in the United States, the World Health Organization Director-General Dr. Ghebreyesus (2020) declared COVID-19 a pandemic on March 11, 2020. Wamsley (2021) described March 11, 2020, as the day everything changed. At the time, the World Health Organization, according to Dr. Atlas (2021), was operating on faulty data. And this flawed data led to significant lapses and delays.

Moreland et al. (2020) noted that March 15 and March 19 were the dates mandatory lockdowns had begun, with a slow trickle across the United States. This means buildings that would usually be filled to a 90 - 95% occupancy began to dwindle below 5 - 10% approximately, only permitting "essential workers," whatever that euphemism means, but includes building engineers, housekeeping, and security personnel (i.e., "*the help*"). Workplace closures impacted 4 out of 5 employees (Rudolph & Zacher, 2021).

With buildings closed since March 15 or operating at a reduced capacity, Ralph B. Lee, Jr., MBA and author of *Is Death So Good That Life Is Bad?* (personal communication, October 25, 2021) noted that infrastructure valuations have changed (i.e., the capitalization rate), including insurance pure risk evaluations. Bhanot (2020) noted that inherit in the demand to ease social distancing bore financial reasons. Therefore, at the heart of many of these required return-to-work policies rests a dollar sign.

Greed

Fascist attitudes take hold when there are no
social anchors and when the perception grows
that everybody lies, steals, and cares only about
him- or herself. —Madeleine Albright

Coser (1974) called these types of organizations "greedy institutions" (p. 5). Greedy institutions, according to Heery and Noon (2017), include those companies that demand total commitment which can be observed in how such companies convey requests (i.e., demands). Employees' cathectic strength (i.e., mental and emotional) is slowly withered away by such organizations.

Along with the concept of greedy institutions, another concept of greed is closely related to it, which Gavett (2021) styled as "greedy work" (p. 5). Greedy work entails compensating employees "disproportionately more on a per-hour basis when someone works a greater number of hours or has less control over those hours" (Gavett, 2021, p. 5).

Greedy work can be voluntary or involuntary. Here is the kicker, sometimes organizations demand greedy work without the matching compensation. Unfortunately, this gets into the narcissistic organization, but these corporations expect that simply because they provide a job to the employee that—that is enough to demand greedy work.

When considering job embeddedness (i.e., the psychological, social, and financial factors), greedy institutions and greedy work can devastate communities. In the book, *Will*, authors W. Smith and Manson (2021) discussed the power of building a wall, one brick at a time. In like manner, an organization can destroy communities by terminating their people, one at a time. It is destabilizing!

Greed Overdrive

...there is no torrent like greed. – Siddharta
Gautama

Organizations were already greedy, but such greed went into overdrive in the 1970s. The 1970s is when the gross domestic product (GDP) calculations changed, and deregulation began to unfurl (Mazzucato, 2018).

Deregulation and privatization became the dominant tools for addressing many of capitalism's flaws (R. D. Wolff, 2021). With such changes, Jaffe (2021) opined how "new work ethics and new spirits of capitalism" formed as these market changes occurred (p. 12), creating what Fraser (2017) styled as "boundary struggles" (p. 154). New work ethics and new spirits of capitalism serve to discombobulate employees, you know, to keep employees from asking questions and making demands on corporations.

Reich (2020) noted that we should be asking "whom the market has been organized to serve" (p. 6). Who benefits? Based on the method and manner of the power dynamics considering the mass terminations, the optics show clearly who benefits, corporations, every time, especially the greedy ones, every time.

Narcissism

Since 'the society' has no future, it makes
sense to live only for the moment, to fix our eyes
on our own 'private performance,' to become
connoisseurs of our own decadence, to cultivate
a 'transcendental self-attention.' – Christopher
Lasch

The notion of greedy institutions was subsequently followed up by Downs (1997), who noted the characteristics of a "narcissistic organization" (p. 12). Narcissistic behavior is not only unhealthy for organizations but also for an organization's employees. For example, narcissistic organizations often seek out, according to Hales et al. (1995), 'yes men.'

The Devastation of Yes Men

"Yes men" can be devastating to organizational culture, lowering the morale of their cohorts within an organization. Indeed, unethical behavior and disguised policies and procedures are wholly consistent with both greedy institutions and narcissistic organizations.

Chapter 14

The Dynamics of Greedy Institutions and Narcissistic Organizations

"HATE IS THE COMPLEMENT OF
FEAR AND NARCISSISTS LIKE
BEING FEARED. IT IMBUES THEM
WITH AN INTOXICATING
SENSATION OF OMNIPOTENCE." —
SAM VAKNIN

"Earth provides enough to satisfy every man's needs, but not every man's greed." —Mahatma Gandhi

The features of narcissistic behavior, according to Ronningstam (2014), include:

- acting pompous;
- living in a fantastical world based upon boundless brilliance, power, or success;
- exhibiting a sense of entitlement;
- using interpersonally exploitative behaviors;
- presenting a lack of empathy; and
- showing arrogant, haughty behaviors.

Features of the greedy, according to de Vries (2016), include:

- exhibiting overly self-centeredness,
- presenting envious behaviors,
- showing a lack of empathy,
- presenting unsatisfied-style behaviors,
- demonstrating manipulative behaviors, and
- showing a need to focus on immediate needs while leaving the calamity for others to address.

Chapter 15

Dealing with the Organizations: Up Close and Personal

"It was impossible to tame, like leeches."
—Lemony Snicket

Gray (as cited in Hutzler, 2021), said that she "'tried everything possible" to maintain her job, even proposing to be tested weekly, yet her request was summarily denied ("Meggan Gray," para. 2). If truth be told, nothing will please greedy institutions and narcissistic organizations other than acclaim, admiration, and the dollar. Accordingly, everything that Gray described fits the greedy and narcissistic patterns demonstrated by these organizations.

What Dignity?

The psychopath regards his [or her] need and
gratifications as infinitely more important than
others'. His [or her] needs and gratifications
always trump the dignity and security of others'.
—Steve Becker

For Gray, however, it was about dignity. Not too many people can stand on their dignity today, because, they do not have any, since their dignity has been slowly siphoned away, which according to Sutton (2007), is encroached through small but cumulative and demeaning acts. Certainly, there is a danger in losing one's dignity.

Losing One's Self

Dehumanization is the belief that some being
only appear human, but beneath the surface,
where it really counts, they aren't human at all.
—David Livingstone Smith

Kierkegaard (2019) noted that "the greatest danger, that of losing one's own self, may pass off as quietly as if it were nothing" (p. 341).

Heying and Weinstein (2021) explained that between cognitive dissonance and the rate of change in our world, we cannot keep up or protect ourselves. So, we check out. Check out from making critical decisions and life. Life just happens with no direct input.

Heying and Weinstein (2021) also noted that people have been disconnected from their interwoven communities and lack local understanding. With this disconnection, it becomes easier to dismiss others, even when the people we are dismissing are a part of our community. Hence, when there is no connection or foundation it becomes easy to rob people of their dignity.

Losing one's dignity also means losing one's common humanity. Functioning without common humanity represents the zone where all the nasty things occur such as the case with Gray and others, reduced work-life balance, and all the other hurts and pains that accumulate in organizations. Hicks (2018) noted that dignity represents common humanity and that everyone desires to be regarded in an equal and equitable manner.

Chapter 16

The Rulers and the Ruled

"THE URGE TO SAVE HUMANITY
IS ALMOST ALWAYS ONLY A
FALSE-FACE FOR THE URGE TO
RULE IT. POWER IS WHAT ALL
MESSIAHS REALLY SEEK: NOT THE
CHANCE TO SERVE." —HENRY
LOUIS MENCKEN

*"Gathering matters because it is through each
other that we figure out what we believe." —
Priya Parker*

Drucker (1978) wrote about a book titled *Management & Machiavelli*, he noted that the underlying premise of the book suggests that the guidelines of the princes and rulers are entirely appropriate for an organization's executives. With executives practicing standards prescribed by the princes and rulers, it only becomes natural that all the leaders and managers of an organization practice such social behavior.

Grant (2021b) noted that few people can escape the lure from the values of others. Polsky (as cited in Balch, 2021) noted that "the behavior of those around you can have more influence on decision making than science and data" ("Dig in their heels," para. 8). That is, according to Polsky (as cited in Balch, 2021), "science and data are not sufficient to influence rational behavior" ("Dig in their heels," para. 8).

According to Brooks (2011), "we become who we are in conjunction with other people becoming who they are" (p. 12). Thus, people's sense of reality is not only formed through their environment but also by what others say and think about them (May, 2009).

What is worse, our beliefs about ourselves can influence our whole life (Aarssen, 2019), and the lives of others. The greatest disadvantage, however, rests with humans' proneness to embrace everyone else's inappropriate and often unsuitable solution (Merton, 2002). When it comes to corporations following unsustainable solutions, the practices are compounded because organizations touch so many people's lives in a variety of ways (Szekely et al., 2017).

Chapter 17

The Fireworks have Begun

There's a movement going down in America.
It's called moving people, from one position to
another. And it's not a fast move. It's going to
take time. —Barry White

The COVID-19 pandemic has had profound implications on organizations and employees (Rudolph & Zacher, 2021). Companies are eager for the employees to come back to physical buildings (Harfoush, 2021). Not only organizations but also some local governments such as New York City have laid pressure down for a return to the office (Egan, 2022).

Employers' eagerness for employers to return to the office center on two main issues: capitalization rates and what Lufkin (2021) styled as "presenteeism" (para. 1). Presenteeism involves "being physically in your seat at work just to look dedicated, no matter how unproductive (Lufkin, 2021, para. 1). The government's interest in employees returning to the office is public image and taxation, not health. Closed office space does not look good for Mayor Eric Adams, New York City's newly elected mayor.

Inherent in the return to work rests an underlying problem. The problem was summed up with one word by Barrero et al. (2022): Density. With many people congregating in old, outdated buildings with poor ventilation, office density becomes a major source of concern and discomfort for employees.

Since the summer of 2020, however, lockdown orders have been rescinded and many organizations are now recalling employees (Arnow-Richman, 2021).

Return-to-work policies have already begun to backfire, especially with employees seeking more autonomy within the workplace. According to Reisinger and Fetterer (2021), for example, 77% of respondents prefer to work for companies that recognize their autonomy to work from anywhere.

Research has suggested that an executive-employee disconnect exists regarding return-to-work policies, creating a gulf between what executives and employees desire (Sarasohn, 2021). The rush to return may be doing more damage than good (Harfoush, 2021).

Conti (as cited in MIT SMR Strategy Forum, 2021) stated:

While relaxing the rules about physical presence may meet workers' desire for more flexibility, it risks hampering face-to-face interactions, which have been found to play a fundamental role in fostering innovation and productivity. Employee productivity and firm performance may suffer as a result. ("Disagree," para. 1)

Productivity Loss is a Fiction

Significant sections of the public are listening uncritically to what corporations tell them and taking it at face value. This is nothing less than a national education emergency. —David Mitchell

Many factors influence remote work. Aspects of remote work can be influenced by a myriad of factors such as assignment contents, digital literacy, household responsibilities, and proper workspaces, to name some (Senatori & Spinelli, 2021). Even with family commitments and other issues, employees' remote work productivity has been shown to remain high through employers' mitigation efforts such as communication and managerial support (Shambi, 2021).

Keeping employees' remote work productivity at parity with in-office work is done through things that organizations should already be doing with employees such as communication. Keeping productivity high and employees involved may require modifying the operating model, but companies can operate and transact business remotely (P. Hudson, 2021).

Face-to-Face Meetings

Again, in spite of their many questions and objections, no one bothered to say anything. — Patrick M. Lencioni

For those who use face-to-face meetings as a means to get back into the office, according to Whillans et al. (2021), meetings were being held for six general reasons: (a) commitment devices, (b) egocentric bias (selfish urgency), (c) fear of missing out (FOMO), (d) meeting amnesia, (e) pluralistic ignorance, and (f) the mere urgency effect. Notice, the closest on the list to move a company's agenda forward is commitment devices. Thus, face-to-face meetings are a poor excuse to force employees to come back to the office. The office, according to Neeley (2022), should be viewed as a tool with defined and specific purposes.

Technology in the Workplace

When people adopt technology, they do old things in new ways. When people internalize technology, they find new things to do. —James McQuivey

Conti's argument is contextual and is not representative of the full spectrum of work-life. Remote work, for example, has become widespread internationally (Shambi, 2021) and is expected to increase (Senatori & Spinelli, 2021). If the truth is told, even when employees are in a physical work environment today, physical interactions have virtually disappeared with the use of technology such as Google Meet, Skype for Business, Zoom, conference calls, emails, and group texts. Organizations have benefited from the research and development of technology, and now, it can facilitate remote work environments at scale (Mitchell, 2021). Deloitte (2021) noted that technology and return-to-work approaches go together. Thus, technology use is imperative to successfully reopening the economy (Lamneck, 2020).

Technology use is the reality of the physical work environment, and it has been for some time. It has been noted, for example, that "if you stop checking your work email, this would harm your career" (Newport, 2019, p. 64). Most often, everything is handled in email services such as Gmail (Newport, 2021). Thus, when people argue about return-to-work policies and how it benefits social interactions, these types of arguments must be taken with a grain of salt, because they are truly disingenuous.

Chapter 18

America's Heartbeat is Suffering

On many days, I feel as if I have no space left in my heart for another grief, no holding pen for the overflow of tears. —Cicely Tyson

A slew of media personalities, for example, either stepped aside or were terminated recently: Karl Bohnak (30 years of service), Meggan Gray (18 years of service), and Kerri Hayden (25 years of service), to designate a few (Hutzler, 2021).

Media personalities were mentioned but terminations are sweeping across the United States like the pandemic itself to everyday, working-class Americans (i.e., the heartbeat of America). The removal of work includes hard-working Americans like Bridgett Penick, a nurse practitioner, (22 years of service) who was removed from the schedule, and Michelle Tanner, a nurse practitioner, who was also removed from the schedule, all because they have refused to follow the vaccine mandate from their employer (ABC 4 Utah, 2021).

Americans are hurting, feeling angry, anxious, depressed, empty, isolated, stressed, stuck, uncertain, and upset (Parker-Pope et al., 2021). These feelings are compounded for the terminated, unvaccinated employees, not necessarily from their vaccination status, but because of the outright unmerited microaggression and venom directed at them.

S. Taylor (2021) noted that the reality of a pandemic's social devastation can hit hard, including arousing financial hardships and stressors that hold a similar impact as the underlying pandemic itself. Financial hardships and stress can hit the vulnerable and underserved hard and swiftly, drying up hope with its devastation.

Chapter 19

Conformity

It is no measure of health to be well adjusted
to a profoundly sick society. —Jiddu
Krishnamurti

Conformity is hard to resist, especially when you already know, your tribesmen will expel you from the tribe. May (2009) said that "since the dominant values for most in our society are being liked, accepted and approved of, much anxiety in our day comes from the threat of not being liked, being isolated, lonely or cast off" ("What is Anxiety," para. 7).

According to Smith (2021), for many of the unvaccinated holdouts, leaving a job has an expensive price tag, one with which the cost may be too high to fathom. Downs (as cited in Balch, 2021) noted that "there comes a point where these incentives [are getting] higher and higher and higher until people just can't afford to not get the vaccine. It does work, but it comes at a cost" ("The stick is more powerful than the carrot," para. 7).

After all, *what is there to lose when the next event comes, and the demand is higher.*

Obedience

It [obedience] is the dispositional cement that
binds men [and women] to systems of authority.
—Stanley Milgram

Conformity is one thing, obedience is another. Employees owe employers what attorneys call the duty of obedience to the directives of the employer as a portion of the application of the work. Fromm (2010) noted that "if a man can only obey and not disobey, he is a slave" (p. 4). Employees represent "slaves in all but name" (Blackmon, 2008, p. 2).

To sum up Lenin (2021), employees represent "wage slaves" in an imperialist system, making employees the 'booty' for all with binding interest to control and divide ("Preface to the French and German Edition, II," paras. 4-5).

Employees have been unwitting slaves, shackled by "an economic slump" (Krugman, 2009, p. 15), "lies about supply and demand" (Sowell, 2009, p. 7), and a lack of "economic dignity" (Sperling, 2020, p. xiv). R. D. Wolff (2021) noted that employers have made off like bandits while employees have been left holding a nearly empty bag. This employer-employee cycle has played out over the last 50 plus years (R. D. Wolff, 2021). Even worse, organizations demand blind obedience, get vaccinated, or else.

Indeed, the or else is always concerning. When the or else sets in, cognitive dissonance (i.e., a psychological vortex that triggers a person to question current beliefs against new beliefs) comes into play. But organizations do not desire employees to hold cognitive dissonance, they seek automatonic responses. And if employees cannot update their programming fast enough, employers seek upgrades, new employees, but in this case, the new employees must come pre-vaccinated for COVID-19.

Organizations, including their bedfellows, are using people's general ignorance of science like what happened to the newly released slaves that were forced into sharecropping, at their own expense, after being freed from slavery.

Shame

We were creating a world where the smartest way to survive is to be blind. —Jon Ronson

If employees will not conform, organizations shame them. According to Burgo (2018), collective sanctions provided a means to control the antisocial behavior of a tribe by shaming its members to promote the maintenance of the group. Thus, terminating employees to curtail group behavior is not a new phenomenon, but it is wholly inconsistent with public policy today.

But then, it is consistent with the not enough culture our society demands of workers today, especially feelings of not being significant enough, which, according to B. Brown (2013), represents the largest initiate of shame within the workplace.

"When we are exposed without any way to protect ourselves, we feel the pain of shame. If we are continually overexposed, shame becomes toxic" (Bradshaw, 2010, p. 10). The terminated, unvaccinated employees have been shamed before their former coworkers. Shamed before their families. Shamed before their communities. Shamed before the world. Organizations have exposed the unvaccinated to toxic shame.

Chapter 20

From the Experience of the Help

"Turn your wounds into wisdom." —Oprah Winfrey

On Friday, July 30, 2021, email inboxes lit up after receiving a message from Bill, Project Manager, Allied Universal Security Services at the World Bank Group headquartered in Washington, D.C. The email read in part: "We'd like to inform you of new [sic] requirement of contractors working at all World Bank properties beginning September 7, 2021" (W. Johnson, personal communication, July 30, 2021).

After receiving this email from Bill, many security officers and Special Police Officers working at the World Bank Group decided to leave. Security Officer Verma was one of the employees who decided to leave. Verma provided 30-plus years of service to the World Bank Group. Verma's story is seared in my mind, which is why it is mentioned here. Even though I was in the throes of being terminated too, I empathized with Verma's story since I discovered the length of his employment and the conditions to which his employment was terminated.

The World Bank Group nor Allied-Universal Security Services did not care about me, my family, my service, or my life. All I could hear in my mind was: this is just business. I recall reading on Allied-Universal Security Services' About Us webpage: "An unrelenting focus on clients' success creates partnerships rooted in quality and value and is supported by experience gained from our years in business" (para. 3). Every time I think about that statement, I shake my head and know Allied-Universal would do anything for a dollar, including lying. My grandmother, Katie, always warned me that if you would lie, you would steal or kill. It is a downward spiral.

It does not matter what state one works for Allied-Universal Security Services, the stories of coverup and deceit are universal from one employee to another (12 News, 2019; Dorrian, 2021). Although the Allied-Universal Security Services is not BBB accredited, their ranking, if the company was accredited, is a 1 out of 5 (Better Business Bureaus (BBB), n.d.).

I was qualified for the position. I was very well educated. I was not pulled from a sideshow in a P. T. Barnum spectacle. I had worked in the position for three years, consistently. For my scheduled shifts, I had shown up promptly, happy to be there and happy to serve others. While in the position, I had no major incidents on which I was not able to handle or solve. *I had facilitated snobbish social gatherings such as Christmas, Thanksgiving, and other special functions without incident, just so the who's who could hobnob. But in the end, my life and my service remained like a ghost with no voice.* I was terminated without a blink of an eye.

I realize the entrenched indifference against today's employees is palpable. We can get lost in the mounds of books written on the subject. *It is one thing reading about it. Yet another to experience the sledgehammer and the callous, coldhearted disregard from organizations to which you have served, diligently. As children, we have been universally trained about not touching hot things. Then, they burn you. And because of the type of system to which we work, like children, we must return to workplaces repeatedly, because our life measures are universally attached. Burned and scorched our whole lives. We work for organizations so we can have a decent retirement, which all too often we never get to appreciate. Our bodies are tired. Our minds are weary. Our souls cry out.*

Empathy Deficit

Empathy's most important role, though, is to inspire kindness our tendency to help each other, even at a cost to ourselves. —Jamil Zaki

Even trees empathize with other trees, so if one cannot feel some level of empathy there is some there-there. These types are called psychopaths and sociopaths (Fritzon et al., 2019; Stout, 2020).

CEOs, leaders, and managers with psychopathy show deficient empathy. Diminished empathy indicates a decreased openness to the distress signals of employees, including the terminated, unvaccinated employees, which ultimately leads to the likelihood that such CEO, leader, or manager will be drawn to respond negatively while others may become aversive to employees distress, even the ones for potential termination (Babiak & Hare, 2009; Blair, 2018). It should be noted that humans are generally risk-averse (Dutton, 2012). Hence, CEOs, leaders, or managers with psychopathic and sociopathic traits are more likely to terminate the unvaccinated employees while also disregarding remaining employees' emotional states and concerns.

Wallisch (2014) noted that "psychopaths treat people like you would treat objects – things to be manipulated for their personal gain with no conceivable ethical or moral dimension" ("Traits of psychopaths," para. 4). Psychopaths are cold, callous, manipulative, lacking remorse while also demonstrating a superficial affect (Morin, 2021). Psychopathic CEOs, leaders, and managers, for example, are the type of people that, in the COVID-19 pandemic, understand the nature of virus mutation but still terminate its employees when there is no effective solution.

These mass COVID-19 terminations are a part of a larger empathy deficit that is sweeping across society.

Arnow-Richman (2021) called it an "acute lack of empathy" (p. 15), which suggests that organizations have only lacked empathy because of COVID-19 issues, which when compared to the method and manner other countries and the United States' organizations addressed the issue, there seems to be a chronic lack of empathy that showed its vicious head. Make no mistake, however, empathy and humility, according to Oghenejobo (as cited in Heskett, 2021), must be a part of an organization's basic values (i.e., which is part of an organization's strategic management model).

The Voice of Reason

It's medication time! — Randle Patrick "R.P." McMurphy, One Flew Over the Cuckoo's Nest

In a letter dated July 30, 2021, I sent to Bill and Rick, Allied-Universal Security Services representatives, discussing the World Bank Group's discriminatory COVID-19 mitigation plan and practices, I wrote: "Indeed, no employee should have to choose between working and giving up his or her dignity to work for a private corporation as considered by the proposed COVID-19 mitigation plan."

For years, the World Bank Group had been preaching one thing, publicly and had been practicing another, privately. The private practices had led to substandard conditions and treatment of contractors, creating a gulf of differences in how permanent "bank staff" and contractors were treated. The treatment of the contractors has produced an ignoble subaltern class.

As COVID-19 marched across the United States, and the lockdowns had begun, the pressure of a pandemic intensified the differences between the World Bank Group's permanent "bank staff" and contractors. The differences prompted me to write about the hypocrisy of the World Bank Group's COVID-19 mitigation strategy.

In effect, the policy of the World Bank Group pursued a plan to only terminate the unvaccinated contractors while giving permanent "bank staff" a pass. When I pointed this elitism, discrimination, and rankism out, Allied-Universal Security Services' management did not appreciate it one bit. But it was the truth, so they had to eat it.

When the original announcement came down concerning terminations, everyone returning to the World Bank Group campus had to be vaccinated, but over time the message had been refined, permanent "bank staff" *would only be encouraged* to get vaccinated. And today, if a permanent "bank staff" shows up unvaccinated, they receive an index card with encouragement on it to get vaccinated, while talking with a contractor the World Bank Group had forced to get vaccinated or be terminated.

In a September 7, 2021, correspondence, I wrote: "For the World Bank Group to receive a public benefit and then arbitrarily select whose inalienable, constitutional, civil, and international rights they will or will not honor and respect makes them gangsters, operating outside the contours of the law, especially the international treaties to which we are signatories."

I had not asked for anything unreasonable. I just wanted to keep my job. I just wanted to make a living. I took a middle-ground approach. So, I needed to understand why my rights were being trampled in the workplace by an organization and people who claim to honor employees' religious expression. I found my answers in a discourse on politics.

Whatever one's political persuasion, when no balance exists, one can be trapped by "mental rigidity" (Cohn, 2019, para. 2). It has been noted that "prejudice is attributable to an ideological conflict that is based on the assumption that people with a different social identity also have different ideological beliefs" (van Prooijen & Krouwel, 2019, pp. 161; 162). Avlon (as cited in Cable News Network (CNN), 2021) summed it up this way: "People with politically extreme beliefs tend to downgrade the humanity and individuality of people with whom they perceive they'll disagree" (section, 3:38 – 3:47).

Mental rigidity and prejudice have played out before the world's watchful eyes. In one state employers are terminating employees for being unvaccinated and in other states, a few states themselves have decided to fight and protect employees from being exposed to mass terminations. Society has fallen into a trap, blinded by prejudice.

When people become blind to reality, it then becomes easy to, for example, dismiss a group of people through an organization's termination process (or put a group of people in gas chambers). Haidt (2012) noted that "people bind themselves into political teams that share moral narratives. Moral narratives are a part of the comfort of tribalism as it helps ease threats (Chua, 2018). Once they accept a particular narrative, they become blind to alternative moral worlds" ("What Lies Ahead," para. 8). In other words, political tribalism takes hold, and as such, when the narrative of the groups is the only thing that is believed, which according to Levy (2020), it is easy to fall into a hatred of others when potential threats are detected, such as employees refusing to get vaccinated.

Mass termination of the unvaccinated represents extremism that would not be tolerated by any other political group.

In this environment, politics exceeded my right to work. Not just my right to work, but all the terminated unvaccinated employees were removed because they sought to express their right to body autonomy. When I say right to work, most people may assume I am off my rocker, but it is a part of one's human right to work. The International Convention on the Elimination of All Forms of Racial Discrimination, which is binding on the United States, guarantees people "the rights to work" (United Nations, 1965, sec. Article 5 (i)).

The workplace is like an authoritarian trap for employees. It has always been that way, the COVID-19 pandemic simply exposes what has been there the entire time. It is in some parts authoritarian. And it is in some parts securitarian (i.e., an unwarranted preoccupation with security).

It is in this vein that I must reflect. I am reminded of the 1980s when music was inclusively played on one radio station, you could listen to rock, jazz, and some hip hop on one channel. You will not find this one-station reality today. Nowadays, however, everyone is being cradled by the safety of securitarian practices, and the worst part is, most do not even realize it. The COVID-19 pandemic uncovered this reality.

Not a Regular Organization

No illusion is more crucial than the illusion
that great success and huge money buy you
immunity from the common ills of mankind... —
Larry McMurtry

The World Bank Group is no regular organization, and if any organization should be following the law, it should be the World Bank Group, because they hold immunity under the International Organizations Immunities Act (IOIA).

N. C. Smith et al. (2021) asked a question: "Does your business need a human rights strategy?" ("Title"). And it is to this question that I would answer in the affirmative. I would even say, hell yes. Then, I would ask: What if the organization is supposed to be a gatekeeper of human rights, how do you address that when they are violating employees' human rights?

My termination resulted from the World Bank Group's COVID-19 mitigation plan. I had requested a legitimate religious accommodation. But the World Bank Group and Allied Universal Security Services were not accepting religious accommodations, medical accommodations, or any other accommodations, regardless of the type.

I found the stance of not accepting religious accommodations inappropriate, especially because of the type of organization the World Bank Group embodies. Even more unacceptable was, getting Allied-Universal Security Services' management to collude in the blanket denial of religious accommodations, which broaches an entirely different level of complicity and violation of the laws of the United States. Not one contract company connected to the World Bank Group received a religious accommodation and neither did any of the contract companies offer accommodations. None of the contract companies were spared from the blanket denial of religious accommodations.

According to the U.S. Equal Employment Opportunity Commission (2002, 2021), there were only two types of accommodations honored for COVID-19: medical and religious. Brackett and Sullivan (2022) noted that "employers must provide a reasonable accommodation to the employee once advised that a policy is in conflict with religious beliefs unless such an accommodation would constitute an undue hardship on the employer" (para. 8).

Tanner (as cited in ABC 4 Utah, 2021) said that "it is absolute BS to have to have an exemption to something that is illegal in the first place" (section, 1:21 – 1:31).

I had emailed my managers Bill and Rick unsuccessfully. When I say unsuccessfully, I mean they did not even respond to any of my emails. On August 30, 2021, I printed out my emails. At the end of my shift, I walked to Bill and Rick's office, and I pushed copies of my emails underneath their door.

On August 31, 2021, the next day, I received an email response from Bill. Bill's email read in part, "You were requested to come see me. You did not" (W. Johnson, personal communication, para. 1, August 31, 2021).

I knew the information in Bill's email was a damn lie. And I wanted him to know I was not accepting his damn lies. So, I intently emailed Bill back, especially to bat down this attempted gaslighting. In my reply to Bill, I wanted him to know I am not stupid. *My mother and grandmother did not send me to school to sit on the stool or for free lunch, they sent me to school to learn.* So, I wrote: "I have not been personally invited to come see you or ever being asked to come see you by either of my supervisors" (S. McCastle, personal communication, August 31, 2021). And Bill knew it. I never thought of Bill to be a half-witted man, but I question why he tried to play me as I was a feebleminded fool.

Gaslighting Everywhere

Gaslighting is a type of manipulation that seeks to sow seeds of doubt in a targeted individual or group, hoping to make targets question their own memory, perception, and sanity. —Janis Bryans

On September 3, 2021, I received an email from Dean. Dean's email stated in part, "Be advised that at this time, the interactive process and/or final determination does exempt you from the client-driven mandate" (D. Daproza, personal communication, para. 3, September 3, 2021).

On September 21, 2021, the date of my termination, I received another email from Dean that read in part: "For the record, you and I never had discussions of your return to World Bank, nor did I gave [sic] you permission/clearance to go back to work" (D. Daproza, personal communication, para. 1, September 21, 2021). Here I am wondering, what the hell!

Just 18 days earlier, Dean had written that I would be "exempt" from the COVID-19 mandate until the World Bank Group and Allied-Universal Security Services worked out the details of my accommodation. Eighteen days is an abbreviated time to forget what was written in a prior email. I am being played. Is he serious? Is this a joke? Does he think I am stupid?

There are a few ways to analyze a situation in which I found myself on September 21, 2021. I know that I was dealing with a few dishonest men, men who would doggedly say anything, at any time. I had been the subject of their deliberate, mendacious act. Here I am, all I am trying to do is work. Trying to earn a living for my family.

What they did not know is that I was well aware of the discussion on bullshitting by Frankfurt (2005), lying by Ekman (2009), and gaslighting by Stern (2007) (i.e., the BLG), all well known. Here is what else I know, we live in a "post-truth era" and I realize it is encapsulated by "an ethical twilight zone" (Keyes, 2004, p. 12), so I understand what to expect by today's standards. Based on the emails from Dean, Bill, and Rick, anyone with a brain can see through the deceit and gaslighting.

It is important to understand that one can tell an untruth without lying (Ekman, 1992). So, I am not talking about untruths without lying. I am referring to those cold, calculated times when someone decides to bullshit or lie. Bergstrom and West (2020) noted that "the world is awash with bullshit, and we're drowning in it" (p. xi).

I had an excellent grasp of the BLG minefield to which I found myself. It was untenable. It was a tricky situation. Continuing to fight an unsustainable fight is like spitting in the wind. I was going to be bullied out, regardless of right or wrong, regardless of the law, regardless of my life or my service.

A Profit in Your Own Home

I assure you and most solemnly say to you, no prophet is welcome in his hometown. —Luke 4:24, Amplified Bible

When one is a voice of reason with no voice at all, people usually call them contrarian. However, Piezunka et al. (2021) noted that while it may seem to be counterintuitive, listening to what contrarians bring to the table can add value. Grant (2021a) noted that "our convictions can lock us in prison of our own making." In many cases, the wisdom of the herd may prevail initially, but contrarian views add to the long-term viability of an organization's plans, especially when they are correct (Piezunka et al., 2021).

What I suggested then and reiterate today is, that people have poured their life into these organizations and to just dump them does not make sense.

In Bill, Rick, and Beyan Bekele's (all managers of Allied-Universal Security Service) rush to meet the World Bank Group's no jab, no job policy, they begin to encourage employees to get the Johnson & Johnson vaccine because it was less time involved and the employees could meet the no jab, no job policy. Rick even sent an email suggesting where Johnson & Johnson vaccines were available. A slew of news organizations and journalists, including Campos (2021) reported that Johnson & Johnson vaccine can lead to a "serious, side effect that has caused blood clots in some people" (para. 1).

A Human Being

His tears proved he was human. —Molly Guptill Manning

Verma is not a Democrat or Republican, he is a human being. As the character, Howard Beale, in the movie *Network* declared: "I'm a human being goddamn it! My life has value!..." (Lumet, 1976, section, 54:30/2:01:18). Everyone knows, but there are a select few who would like to forget, "there is no cure for being human" (Bowler, 2021, p. 187).

No one should have to work for an organization that they must constantly remind the organization that they are human beings, first. But that is exactly what today's employees are being called to do in an ever-changing, global economy. Indeed, employees come to organizations as "humans first, with their own outlooks and values" (Guadalupe et al., 2021, para. 1).

COVID-19 and What Politics?

I'm not a politician, but I know how to politic.
—Lamarkus C. Houston

COVID-19 is not a left or right issue. COVID-19 has no regard for the wealthy or the disadvantaged. For the blue or red. Or for African- or white Americans. Any suggestion to the contrary represents *stinking thinking*. It is important to note, however, that some demographic and socioeconomic groups have been disadvantaged by the practices of COVID-19 mitigation.

A Breakdown of Consciousness

The mind is still haunted with its old unconscious ways... —Julian Jaynes

Arnow-Richman (2021) noted that the demographic and socioeconomic pain were not uniformly spread, attributing the issue to a "failure of law" (p. 3). It has also been a failure of consciousness, a complete breakdown of what is right and wrong. No one had been through a pandemic before, so no one knew exactly what to expect (Nooyi, 2021). Public policy was not clear. Company policy was not clear. But one thing was clear, humans know the difference between right and wrong, and so do these organizations.

Lots of Warning – The Handwriting was on the Wall

It is also a warning. It is a warning that, if nobody reads the writing on the wall, man will be reduced to the state of the beast, whom he is shaming by his manners. —Mahatma Gandhi

Here is the problem with the terminations of Verma and others at Allied-Universal Security Services stationed at the World Bank Group: On September 21, 2021, I provided written notice to Dean, Regional

Human Resource Representative for Allied-Universal Security Services that Biden (2021) had issued an executive order with two COVID-19 options:

> The Department of Labor is developing an emergency rule to require all employers with 100 or more employees, that together employ over 80 million workers, to ensure their workforces are fully vaccinated or show a negative test at least once a week. (para. 28)

Once this announcement came from the White House, about these government edicts, organizations should have begun implementing the supporting infrastructure (Nagele-Piazza, 2021).

Information Avoidance

A great deal of intelligence can be invested in ignorance when the need for illusion is deep.
—Saul Bellow

Despite my warnings and publicly available information about these government edicts (i.e., information avoidance), Dean, Bill, and Rick still authorized terminations of their employees at the prompting of the World Bank Group. I had been told before, this was a "client-driven mandate" (D. Daproza, personal communication, para. 3, September 3, 2021), meaning the World Bank Group did not care about the issues I had raised, and Allied-Universal Security Services did not care either.

When people avoid information they are responsible to receive, organizational liability increases exponentially. This is a phenomenon known as "willful blindness" (Heffernan, 2011, p. 2). Willful blindness occurs when a person possesses an opportunity and responsibility to be informed with information, but dodges the occasion and obligation, leading a person to, for example, consciously deny truths, feelings, or facts (Heffernan, 2011).

After I had already been terminated, On October 6, 2021, Rick, in writing, said: "WBG [World Bank Group] contractors are being required to get tested for COVID...weekly (after next week) same as WBG staff" (W. Lewis, personal communication, paras. 1;3, October 6, 2021).

Before Rick's email, contractors were not allowed to participate in anything the World Bank Group permanent "bank staff" initiated. Before Rick's October 6th email arrived, I had cautioned Dean, Bill, and Rick, in writing, about the World Bank Group's elitist stance toward contractors and COVID-19 mitigation plan. I had no voice. The World Bank Group's caste system was alive and operating well.

Chapter 21

Caste and Rankism in the Workplace

And even if you fall on the privileged side of these traits you can still be treated as a nobody by people who want to make themselves feel superior. —*Robert W. Fuller*

AND MANY OF THEM ARE SO INURED AND SO HOPELESSLY DEPENDENT ON THE SYSTEM THAT THEY WILL FIGHT TO PROTECT IT. MORPHEUS, THE MATRIX

According to Fuller (2004), rankism is the "mother of 'isms'" (Chapter "Mother of 'Isms,'" para. 1). Rankism is a poison pill. Rankism is considered to be a social disorder (R. W. Fuller, n.d.), and forms a predatory practice of our past (R. W. Fuller, 2013). Rankism: It is bad news! Richardson (2003) said that rankism is a "worldwide epidemic of kicking the dog, a perpetual habit of abusing those we perceive as being lower on the ladder and of being abused by those above" (para. 4).

Many people desire a dignitarian workplace. The most salient of rankism is that people will die to ensure rankism's survival (R. W. Fuller, 2004, Chapter "Why Rank Matters," para. 2). To reach such possibilities afforded by dignity within the workplace, organizations must first recognize the caste in their workplace and extinguish rankism. It is a tool, however, one the corporate bully and inadequate leader use well.

Wu (2021b) noted that being fully vaccinated came with a cachet of liberties that no one else enjoyed, including the ability to maintain one's employment. *People who engage in the practices of rankism are never satisfied, which makes rankism cannibalistic and destructive as capitalism.* Here Wu (2021a) made another point about isolating vaccinated people, which underscores the cannibalistic nature of rankism, outgroups, even when they are considered fully vaccinated, can still be the subject of cold hard discrimination in a system of rank.

Changing Meanings

Too narrow a definition tends to complicate
any endeavour. —Steven Redhead

The higher echelon can change the definition of what fully vaccinated means with no repercussions from the masses because people locked into a system of rank hold a misguided belief that they are better off. However, when pulling back the layers of the onion, basic humanity says something otherwise, the higher-ranked people are no better off than anyone else. But they cannot see it because they have chocolate-covered glasses on.

The top echelon is already itching for a change in the definition of what fully vaccinated means (Wu, 2021b). When the government operates from functional definitions (i.e., definitions that they design and can change), what does that mean for rankism? What does that mean for constitutional rights? Government officials can easily change the definition of fully vaccinated and every three months, the government requires employers to ensure the people are fully vaccinated according to the definition that they have established. David (2021b) called it the "shifting definition" (para. 11). Functional definitions are designed from the point of view of the person or corporation that uses it.

Goldman Sachs, for example, is one such employer that will force its employees to get boosted for COVID-19 vaccination (Anthes & Weiland, 2021). What is apparent from this cannibalistic-style approach to definitions is that people who once believed they were fully vaccinated could lose access to all the social benefits that accrued with the original definition of fully vaccinated.

The CDC (2021d) currently defines being fully vaccinated as "a person is considered fully vaccinated against SARS-CoV-2 infection ≥2 weeks after receipt of the second dose in a 2-dose series (Pfizer-BioNTech and Moderna) or ≥2 weeks after receipt of a single dose of the Janssen COVID-19 Vaccine" ("Primary series," para. 2).

In my experience, before my termination, I witnessed first-hand how definition changes are practiced at the World Bank Group and Allied-Universal Security Services. With the CDC protocol in the background, the two organizations initially followed the CDC guidelines, then when these two organizations realized the amount of resistance from employees and how long employees would be off from work, these organizations lowered the standard.

When a new definition is unveiled, the new definition will be something that allows the United States government to avail itself of maximum benefit and so will the corporations follow.

The Message was Presented About Caste

*We human beings seem always to have found
it comforting to have someone to look down on—
a bottom level of fellow creatures who are very
vulnerable, but who can somehow be blamed
and punished for all or any troubles. We need
this lowest class as much as we need equals to
team with and to compete against and superiors
to look to for direction and help. —Octavia E.
Butler*

According to Wilkerson (2020), "America has an unseen skeleton, a caste system that is as central to its operation as are the studs and joists that we cannot see in the physical building we call home" (p. 16). Wilkerson (2021) delivered the same message to the World Bank Group in a chat. With the COVID-19 mitigation plan, the message of casteism seemed to have fallen mute to those who received Wilkerson's 2021 message.

In situations such as the COVID-19 pandemic, the cannibalistic nature of casteism and rankism show their ugly head, whether people notice it is caste or rank. As noted by R. W. Fuller (2004) even on the privileged side, privilege even represents a pseudo-fixture of the structure. Before COVID-19 vaccines were developed, everyone was in the same boat. Following COVID-19 vaccines, the unvaccinated became the scapegoats. When people realized the vaccines waned after two months, the under-vaccinated will become high-value targets (Hill, 2021).

So today, I can report to Ms. Wilkerson that the studs and joists are coming apart. The house has not begun falling from a single act but by an unsustainable system. Now, casteism and rankism may well survive the

COVID-19 pandemic, but even those upper echelons will look at their pseudo- privilege differently, even those who terminated me.

What the COVID-19 pandemic has done to casteism and rankism, one single person could have not accomplished in a lifetime. The COVID-19 has set all human beings at their core humanity, though some attempted to flee and fight it while some simply attempted to blame others.

Chapter 22

The Biden COVID-19 Rules

Measures to control infectious diseases don't need to be coercive and comprehensive. The opposite is true: they work best when they are consensual and precise... —Alex de Waal

According to Hsu (2021), the Biden Administration rolled out two of its rules on November 4, 2021. The rules are as follows: Companies with 100 or more employees have until January 4, 2021, to be fully vaccinated or begin producing negative weekly COVID-19 tests, and while getting tested, employees must be paid to do so (Hsu, 2021).

Among CEOs, the Biden Administration's COVID-19 rules received mixed support (A. Smith, 2021). The mixed support may arise because those CEOs were too busy copying and pasting other organizations' approaches to the COVID-19 pandemic to develop an effective and sustainable approach themselves.

Even some states had disagreed with vaccine mandates, going as far as enacting laws to prevent vaccine mandates in their state. Durkee (2021) noted that to date, Florida has strengthened its ability to bar COVID-19 vaccine mandates. Texas, another state, according to the Associated Press (2021) issued a COVID-19 prohibition against private businesses to prevent enforcement of any COVID-19 related vaccine mandates.

Some companies, however, bucked at the Texas prohibition against the COVID-19 vaccine mandate, eschewing Greg Abbott's, Governor of Texas, order, noting that federal law trumps state law. However, in a twist in the COVID-19 vaccine mandate war, according to Schnell (2021), the Occupational Safety and Health Administration (OSHA) has decided against enforcement, suspending its efforts to implement the Biden Administration's plan to ensure organizations with over 100 employees either receives a COVID-19 vaccine or present a negative weekly test.

The suspension resulted from *BST Holdings v. OSHA 21-60845* (2021) where Judge Engelhardt of the United States Court of Appeals for the Fifth Circuit noted that:

> The Mandate is a one-size-fits-all sledgehammer that makes hardly any attempt to account for differences in workplaces (and workers) that have more than a little bearing on workers' varying degrees of susceptibility to the supposedly 'grave danger' the Mandate purports to address. (p. 8)

The few COVID-19 vaccine bans represent efforts to get on the bandwagon, going in the opposite direction from the private encroachment taking place in other sectors of the country. Companies that have eschewed Texas' ban against COVID-19 vaccines must be walking on eggshells like they had their employees doing over the last few months. Eventually, when the Federal and state courts wake up from their slumber, the silly season will immediately halt.

Get Some Buckets, the Plan is Leaking

Man is born free but everywhere is in chains.
—Jean-Jacques Rousseau

Heyward (2021) and Paybarah and Abelson (2021) reported that two federal courts, the U.S. District Court Western District of Louisiana, Monroe Division, and the U.S. District Court for the Eastern District of Missouri have issued temporary injunctions concerning the Biden administration's COVID-19 mitigation plan.

In the Louisiana case, *State of Louisiana et al. v. Xavier Becerra et al. Case No. 3:21-Cv-03970* (2021), Judge Doughty noted that:

> There is no question that mandating a vaccine to 10.3 million healthcare workers is something that should be done by Congress, not a government agency. It is not clear that even an Act of Congress mandating a vaccine would be constitutional. (pp. 21-22)

Not even an Act of Congress. Those are powerful words. I thought, maybe it was just me, that the ink had dried on the constitution long ago, but maybe I was dreaming. Let me pinch myself. Who knows in an era where anything goes? Not only has Congress not given their assent to the vaccine mandates encroaching Americans' constitutional rights, Bade et al. (2021) reported that Republicans had intended to shutter the government to defund any effort to force vaccination mandates.

In the case of the *State of Missouri et al. v. Joseph R. Biden, Jr., in his official capacity as the President of the United States of America et al. Case No. 4:21-cv-01329-MTS* (2021), Judge Schelp noted that Congress has not provided permission to an agency to force vaccinations. Judge Schelp also noted that the plaintiffs would most likely succeed.

As Paybarah and Abelson (2021) reported, these lower court rulings are likely to be appealed to higher courts, but these two court opinions are quite revealing. As I have noted, when an employee does not hold body autonomy, he or she is chattel property.

In a prior ruling, Judge Engelhardt observed that "the public interest is also served by maintaining our constitutional structure and maintaining the liberty of individuals to make intensely personal decisions according to their own convictions—even, or perhaps particularly, when those decisions frustrate government officials" (*BST Holdings v. OSHA 21-60845*, 2021, p. 20).

In another case, the *State of Georgia, et al., v. Joseph R. Biden, in his official capacity as President of the United States, et al. CIVIL ACTION NO.: 1:21-cv-163* (2021) Judge Baker of the United States District Court for the Southern District of Georgia Augusta Division issued a nationwide injunction against another part of the Biden administration's COVID-19 mitigation plan for federal contractors. Judge Baker wrote:

> In its practical application (requiring a significant number of individuals across the country working in a broad range of positions and in numerous different industries to be vaccinated or face a serious risk of losing their job), it operates as a regulation of public health. It will also have a major impact on the economy at large, as it limits contractors' and members of the workforce's ability to perform work on federal contracts. Accordingly, it appears to have vast economic and political significance. (p. 19)

Ultimately, the judge noted that President Biden has likely exceeded his authority to issue such a mandate (Kimball, 2021c). The Editorial Board (2021) at the Wall Street Journal has declared the Biden administration's plan a complete wipeout, noting that whoever advised the president on a vaccine mandate needs their law license revoked.

In another twist, the United States Senate has voted to use the Congressional Review Act to repeal the Biden administration's vaccination or test mandate, but it is unlikely the United States House of Representatives will consider the measure because it is controlled by

Democrats and even if it were, Biden would likely veto the bill (Barrabi, 2021). Essentially, this kicks the can to the courts, which seem to be waking up from their slumber as their molasses-style reaction has been less inspiring, and even when they did react, their rulings sometimes adversely impacted individual groups of employees or students who sought to have the vaccine mandates overturned.

Sneed (2021a) reported that the 6th US Circuit Court of Appeals, once it acquired jurisdiction, overturned its sister court's ruling from the 5th Circuit Court of Appeals which had blocked the Biden administration vaccine mandate on large employers. This back-and-forth case is headed for a showdown at the United States Supreme Court.

The United States Supreme Court will ultimately rule on the validity of the Biden administration's vaccine or test rules. January 7, 2022, is the date slated for oral arguments of which the warm reception given by lower courts' permissive approach that has allowed vaccine mandates is not expected from the high court (Sneed, 2021b).

In the article, *Congressional Republicans tell Supreme Court to block Biden's 'health police' vaccine mandate,* Olson and Singman (2021) noted that the Congressional Republicans filed a brief with the court arguing that the Occupational Safety and Health Administration (OSHA) has overstepped its authority. OSHA is not the health police, and neither are corporations.

Liptak (2022a) reported that most Supreme Court justices seemed unconvinced at the government's jab or test requirement imposed on private employers and employees. The Biden administration seemed to have overreached in their COVID-19 mitigation efforts (Hodge, 2022).

Liptak (2022b) reported that the United States Supreme Court declined to uphold the Biden administration's jab or test mandate for large employers, but modestly allowed for the vaccine requirement of health care workers at facilities receiving federal subsidies. In the case, *National Federation of Independent Business, et al. v. Department of Labor - Occupational Safety and Health Administration, et al. 595 U. S. _____* (2022), the court noted that OSHA lacked such authority to impose such an employer mandate, noting that "permitting OSHA to regulate the hazards of daily life—simply because most Americans have jobs and face those same risks while on the clock—would significantly expand OSHA's regulatory authority without clear congressional authorization" (p. 7).

After the Biden administration's failed attempt to push their mandate in the face of American workers, the administration withdrew its jab or test mandate (E. Goldberg, 2022).

Ultimately when considering the Biden administration's proposed jab or test requirement, it was a slick way of taxing the unvaccinated (another penalty), because most, if not all, U.S. employers passed those costs onto their employees in one form or another. And where businesses ate the jab or test costs, those expenditures became a tax on those businesses.

Chapter 23

Violating Employees' Autonomy

"Those three things - autonomy, complexity, and a connection between effort and reward - are, most people will agree, the three qualities that work has to have if it is to be satisfying." —
Malcolm Gladwell

Return-to-work policies risk alienating employees. Lamneck (2020) stated that return-to-work policies must not only be viewed as what is good for organizations only, but such policies must consider employees' well-being. Simply putting out return-to-work demands without clear objectives can be just as painful as the underlying COVID-19 pandemic because it can lead to confusion for employees (Nooyi, 2021).

Rock and Pruitt-Haynes (2021) mentioned that "mandates feel like a violation of autonomy, which is one of the most important intrinsic drivers of threat and reward in the brain" ("Why Mandates Feel Like a Threat," para. 1). According to Reisinger and Fetterer (2021), a return-to-work mandate generates a high employee aversion.

To add insult to injury, according to Dowling et al. (2021), "many [return-to-work] announcements to date have been rule-based, inflexible, and have treated remote work as a perk, rather than a pandemic necessity that proved to be quite successful for many" (para. 2).

Remote work provided a widespread emergency stop-gap measure for employers (Senatori & Spinelli, 2021). Even reluctant employers were required to consider remote work options (Ratcliffe & Wilson, 2021). Regardless of employers' intentions, return-to-work policies, post-COVID-19, will be called more and more into question because the way employees work and interact with their workplaces will change, especially with location-independent work (Vijayakumar, 2021). Tanusree and Brennan (2021) stated that remote work is here to stay.

While remote work may be novel to some organizations, both men and women of the United States have been performing remote work since Neil Armstrong's 1969 walk on the moon (National Aeronautics and Space

Administration (NASA), 2019) and continuous remote work since the International Space Station 1998 (International Space Station National Laboratory (ISS), n.d.). Many things can be learned from the 1969 mission and the 1998 mission into outer space. For example, according to Tanusree and Brennan (2021), both organizations and employees must be able to (a) construct new zeitgebers (i.e., natural rhythms for workflow and remote work), (b) plot out different structures and flexibility, and (c) concentrate on core communication competencies.

There are many factors to consider about the future of work (Cappelli, 2021), returning to the office is just one element. Another side of the return to the office approach rests with stripping employees of the newly acquired flexibility.

If you are the type of CEO that only believes that employees need to come back into an office is an effective strategy, then the board needs to start looking for your replacement now. According to Pisani (2021) and Westerman (2021), post-COVID-19 work requires systemic change in all organizations' leaderships' mindsets. This includes not only reducing pressure off office employees but also removing tension from physical work to avoid the haves and have nots in the workplace (Nooyi, 2021). After all, companies should not be creating two tiers even when there is remote work (P. Hudson, 2021).

The Great Resignation

All over the place, from the popular culture to the propaganda system, there is constant pressure to make people feel that they are helpless, that the only role they can have is to ratify decisions and to consume. —Noam Chomsky

Looking at systems, big data, and the internet of things (IoT), the knowledgeable people (i.e., CEOs, leaders, and managers) knew today's workplace is not compatible with the fast pace, client-centered, action-focused clients' world of information. Organizations already know, to keep up with stepped-up changes complex systems produce, they must adjust and evolve their strategies (Lenderman & Langham, 2019).

The constant drive for output in today's workforce is a relic, a leftover from the Industrial Revolution (Harfoush, 2019; Ressler &

Thompson, 2015). Yet, companies continue to pile on. Something was bound to break down somewhere. This type of workplace pressure cooker is disruptive to what employees value most (Weisinger & Pawliw-Fry, 2015).

It is no wonder why we have a "Great Resignation" (Klotz, 2021; K. L. Miller, 2021; Washington Post Live, 2021), an employee-driven phenomenon unexpected (Gratton, 2021). Employees have had enough. Because "the way we're working isn't working in our own lives, for the people we lead and manage, and for the organizations in which we work" (Schwartz et al., 2010, p. 4). Moreover, organizations know the current workplace is not working for its employees.

Companies have returned to their usual status quo, regardless of a pandemic and irrespective of the workforce. Gipson-Fine (2022) noted that despite all the loss and grief, organizations have failed to adjust to employees' emotional requirements. *Organizations have hedged their bets that they will have a higher chance of obtaining an attitudinal response rather than a behavioral response from employees* (and my research on loss and grief bears this finding out). Barry et al. (2021) noted that for other mandates such as the flu, employees who represented that they would leave their job did not follow through.

Top-down, power-hungry, narcissistic organizations are leading the charge to return, readily, to the same old and outdated approaches. Employers are attempting to create pre-pandemic legibility and it seems not to be working on employees anymore. For example, Casselman (2022) noted that in November 2021, 4.5 million and in October 2021, 4.2 million employees voluntarily separated from their workplace, noting that this is the highest increase over a 20-year cycle since such employment data has been monitored. Employers cannot get a handle on it partly because the workforce lacks trust in its systems.

At the heart of the Great Resignation lies three fundamental truths about employees, according to Gratton (2021): (a) employees have become multistage voyagers seeking flexibility (i.e., life has become more than a ride from cradle to the grave), (b) employees have more room for risk, and (c) employees have begun to exercise their personal agency. These three factors combined will make it more difficult to attract or maintain employees without these considerations in mind. Ultimately, companies are being nudged to become better (Neeley, 2022).

Part 3

Chapter 24

Merry-Go-Round: AIDS and COVID-19

"The problem with the idea that history repeats itself is that when it isn't making us wiser it's making us complacent." —Lisa Halliday

It is déjà vu! The COVID-19 pandemic feels like the AIDS epidemic of the 1980s all over again, just on a larger scale. Horowitz and Martin (2018) noted that the origin of HIV has been shrouded in secrecy. COVID-19 is known to have originated in Wuhan, China, but the exact source of the pathogen is less known. AIDS has been described as the most feared pathogen (Horowitz & Martin, 2018), but today, COVID-19 is the most feared virus.

Unfortunately, we are still living with the ramifications of the 1980s, and unbelievably, once our favored political candidate is booted from office (Democrat or Republican), our children and grandchildren will be faced with the same myriad geopolitical issues.

Novel pathogens can be identified, confined, and examined at amazing speeds today (Ridley & Chan, 2021). Despite new technological advances and surveillance, whether it is today, five years ago, or 20 years ago, society is still unable to prevent pandemics (S. Taylor, 2021).

No one knows where or when, but according to Gottlieb (2021), the world will experience another pandemic. This gets to the heart of the issues of mass terminations as a severe policy deficit. Instead of addressing the policy deficit, the government including the private sector has chosen to scapegoat the most vulnerable. Campbell (2012) noted that blame has steadily become a significant commodity and those who traffic in it have discovered its extraordinarily profitable properties.

COVID-19 and HIV Mutations

A virus is a piece of bad news wrapped in protein. —Sir Peter Medawar

One of the things that we learned in the 80s and 90s from the AIDS epidemic is that "AIDS vaccines able to fight any HIV strain have thus far eluded science. HIV frequently mutates its coat protein, dodging vaccine makers' efforts to elicit sufficiently broadly neutralizing antibodies" (Fliesler, 2016, para. 1).

With COVID-19 mutations, we have seen multiple mutations: Alpha, Beta, Delta, and Omicron. Pathogens mutate regularly, but generally, such mutations do not alter their underlying behavior, and when the basic behavior of a virus does change its regular behavior, it is assigned a Greek letter and becomes a variant of concern such as Omicron which represents a variant and a strain (K. V. Brown, 2021). With this assessment, the efficacy of one type of vaccine will not remain effective for each mutation of COVID-19.

Classifications include (a) variant of interest, (b) variant of concern, and (c) variant of high consequence (Bollinger & Ray, 2021).

Bollinger and Ray (2021) noted:

- A *variant of interest* has a genetic footprint that foretells higher transmissibility, immunity escape, or more consequential disease.
- A *variant of concern* has a footprint that is more likely to result in immunity and vaccine escape in the previously vaccinated and previously infected. A variant of concern comes with features such as high transmissibility, more consequential disease, and resistance to antiviral therapeutics.
- A *variant of high consequence* currently has no vaccines and no defense.

American Cheese

In the event that I am reincarnated, I would like to return as a deadly virus, to contribute something to solving overpopulation. Prince Philip, Duke of Edinburgh

The COVID-19 vaccine program is like President Reagan's "government cheese" program. The government needed to save face, so they found a creative way to get rid of the cheese from a program that had been initiated by President Carter. So, the government pushed out the cheese.

According to Malone and Duffin (2021), the "government cheese" program all started with a campaign promise in 1976. Once President Carter was dethroned, President Reagan was left with the bag. Remember, COVID-19 economic and social effects began under President Trump. AIDS' economic and social effects began under President Reagan.

According to Karp (2018), the United States government began stockpiling dairy products, including cheese, in the 30s, and at some point, the warehouses had become overrun with cheese. Buying milk was off the table (Malone & Duffin, 2021). Those who received the cheese, depending on their viewpoint, were either filled with gratitude or shame (Blakemore, 2018).

Instead of cheese today, the government is now pushing vaccines. And when the United States government financed the cheese, at a price tag of about 2.5 billion dollars, they now desired their cut from Moderna (Rutschman, 2021).

Although the vaccine efficacy is not what was advertised, the underlying research is still important, however.

New Zealand reported a death linked to the Pfizer COVID-19 vaccine, yet the Pfizer COVID-19 vaccine remains safe (Beals, 2021). Johnson & Johnson vaccine is known to cause blood clots, yet the CDC announced they would allow Johnson & Johnson to remain on the market (Robbins & Jewett, 2021). In comparison to the polio vaccine in the 1950s, Fitzpatrick (2006) noted that the polio vaccine killed 10 children and left about 200 with differing levels of immobilization. Following the children's deaths from the polio vaccine, the United States government ordered the polio vaccine recall (Ruane, 2020). This is in stark contrast to the government's response to the COVID-19 vaccines.

Since authorizing children to receive the COVID-19 vaccines, reports of elevated risk of myocarditis, heart problems, have received attention in recent studies (Mevorach et al., 2022). Mandavilli (2022b) reported that the numbers from the recent study in children are in tension with the number from the CDC.

Treisman (2021) reported that a Norwegian Cruise Lines ship with 3,200 fully vaccinated souls aboard was placed on lockdown when an outbreak of COVID-19 occurred. The cruise ship outbreak follows an uptick in breakthrough COVID-19 infection as reported by Fortier (2021) with a 44% increase and as Aravindan and Lin (2021) noted with an uptick of 75%.

This COVID-19 outbreak flies in the face of government-backed vaccine mandates, but politicians keep pushing this Chinese ideology on the American people. The government cheese program was to reduce the level of cheese in its warehouses, the government did not care how the cheese was reduced, but it was still marketed as a humanitarian program.

On December 30, 2021, 24 days after Treisman (2021) reported a COVID-19 outbreak, the CDC (2021e) changed its cruise ship guidelines for all would-be passengers, even those who are fully vaccinated, should avoid cruises. The CDC's change in posture does not bode well for office spaces, but corporations will continue to insist, over time, that employees return to the office to meet the capitalization rate.

Worldwide reports of the vaccinated people still being contaminated with COVID-19 should give pause on the vaccine programs, but the government and some private corporations are still pushing these vaccines. Yoon (2021) reported that South Korea is one of the most vaccine-compliant countries worldwide, and yet the South Koreans cannot reduce the spread of Covid-19. For example, even after receiving the initial COVID-19 vaccine and getting boosted, Marisa Fotieo found herself isolated in a plane's bathroom for three hours, positive with COVID-19 (Smart & Ravindran, 2021).

Liu et al. (2021) noted that "even a third booster shot may not adequately protect against Omicron infection" (p. 7). "Oh yeah, keep getting jabbed with low efficacy COVID-19 vaccine."

If many people were less enthused to get vaccinated, many will be even less enthusiastic to receive a booster shot. S. Hubler and Harmon (2021) reported that of all the adults eligible for a booster, only around 30% have received one. To keep the pressure on people, a definition change is on the horizon to pressure people into receiving more vaccines.

Now, the United States government has authorized the mixing and matching of vaccines as boosters (Zimmer, 2021), both heterologous boosting and homologous boosting (Fryhofer, 2021). This approach is like your doctor saying take Acetaminophen, Aspirin, and Ibuprofen, and "call me in the morning," especially because the CDC has used "neutral and vague" language to authorize this approach (Fryhofer, 2021, "Transcript," para. 8).

And it is with this understanding that the American taxpayers are being bamboozled, had, hosed, swindled, and taken for a ride.

The COVID-19 cheese has gotten expensive for Americans, and those who seem to raise objections seem to be treated as bumbling fools. Jeong and Suliman (2021) and Kimball (2021d) reported that Albert Bourla, Pfizer's CEO, had forecast that a fourth jab of the COVID-19 vaccine may be needed after a third dose.

Israel authorizes its fourth COVID-19 vaccine dose for the most vulnerable (Heller, 2021) and countrywide for its entire population (Morris, 2022), and the United States cannot be too far behind in such a push to get people vaccinated. Although Israel authorized its fourth dose of COVID-19 vaccines, new research suggested that the results of a fourth jab produced slack results (Federman, 2022). In other words, pushing the fourth jab or subsequent jabs from the vaccine's current lot demonstrates low efficacy. And the continuation of such an approach only demonstrates that these pharmaceutical companies are dictating public policy in an effect to continue pushing out the cheese.

Nathan-Kazis (2022) noted that European health officials are holding up a red flag on too many booster shots. Too much and too fast characterizes the vaccine mitigation plan.

Dr. Marco Cavaleri, head of Biological Health Threats and Vaccine Strategy for the European Medicines Agency, (as cited in European Medicines Agency, 2022) said that "repeated vaccinations within short intervals would not represent a sustainable long-term strategy" (Section, 07:27 - 07:36). Again Dr. Cavaleri (as cited in European Medicines Agency, 2022) further noted that "once, or maybe twice [represents acceptable booster doses], but it's not something that we think should be repeated constantly" (Section, 23:35 – 23:42).

It is also important to note that Dr. Cavaleri's warnings are not coming from the Biden administration, particularly the CDC, and many state agencies because such warnings do not fit their vaccine strategy and public narrative.

It has been pointed out and widely expected that people who desire vaccine-injected protection will ultimately be getting jabbed for COVID-19 about three to four times a year (Dr. Reality - Dave Champion, 2021). Unfortunately, mRNA vaccine durability wanes at about two months (Chemaitelly et al., 2021; Y. Goldberg et al., 2021). But when news comes out about the unacceptable nature of repeated injections for COVID-19, instead of changing their approach, the United States government and corporate America have doubled down.

So, is it unrealistic, now, to stand on a United States battleship and declare war on COVID? After all, we know how ineffective the war on drugs has been.

Chapter 25

Demagogues and COVID-19

Silverman (as cited in Vitka, 2021) questioned religious exemptions for vaccinations, asking: "Why should we keep the religious exemption?" (para. 2). It is this type of intolerance and indifference for employees' significance that drives such disrespect and incivility in the workplace. Such bigotry itself is intolerable in a free society, especially from government representatives. This type of apathy and small-mindedness stems from what West (as cited in Harvard Graduate School of Education, 2017) called a "spiritual blackout, which is the relative eclipse of integrity, honesty, decency, and generosity" (section, 21:05 – 21:16).

Unfortunately, spiritual blackout degrades the ethic of care all humans are called upon to honor. Questioning one's religious exemptions is no different than what other demagogues do. The agenda that is truly being pushed is neoliberalism. Fullbrook and Morgan (2021) noted that the world is in crisis, and neoliberalism has a multifaceted role. Collier (2018) observed that society is coming unglued. Core neoliberalism is designed to accomplish one thing: to make the rich, richer and the poor, poorer (Dasic, 2021).

Jaffe (2021) noted that underlying neoliberalistic thought advances a persuasive allure which is: price tags should be appended to everything. This type of thinking means, get back to work, you are chattel property, as soon as possible, by any means necessary. This type of environment creates a "just f*ucking do it" approach to business (Hibbert, 2019). Ethics, out the door. Humanity, out the door. Morality, out the door. "Just f*ucking do it." Baker (2016) said:

> Markets are never just given. Neither God nor nature hands us a worked-out set of rules determining the way property relations are defined, contracts are enforced, or macroeconomic policy is implemented. These matters are determined by policy choices. The elites have written these rules to redistribute income upward. Needless to say, they are not eager to have the rules rewritten – which means they also have no interest in even having them discussed. (p. 8)

After dealing with the World Bank Group and Allied-Universal Security Services, my first-hand experience affirms that the elites do not and will not hold a conversation. And when it comes down to it, they will terminate its employees to maintain their status.

Personal chattel can be animate or inanimate (Black, 1990), and in this case, it is the employees of these corporations. Personal chattel means these corporations own their employees, and they know it.

West (as cited in Harvard Graduate School of Education, 2017) noted that "the neoliberal soul-craft, the obsession with smartness, the obsession with money, and the obsession with bombs" is what today's society is experiencing (section, 21:17 – 21:26). Neoliberal soul-craft can corral and corner anyone who experiences it, psychologically, into a false consensus effect.

Ross et al. (1977) noted that false consensus can occur anytime anyone observes social behavior. Choi and Cha (2019) stated that people are apt to identify their attitudes, behaviors, beliefs, and decisions to be more ubiquitous than they are. This behavior can certainly be attributed to miseducation.

Unfortunately to such miseducation, Gregory (as cited in Reel Black, 2021) said that when you "teach me to respect filth, you make me think there's something wrong with me" (section, 39:59 – 40:04). We do not know our true selves because we spend so much time dealing with the archetypes and construction of social, private, and intimate selves that we fail to understand our true selves (Chopra, 2021). Therefore, as such identity issues crop up, society can anticipate a ramp-up in psychosocial health issues including anxiety, depression, grief, and PTSD resulting from the return-to-work adhesion policies that abound without the appropriate psychological safety.

While the People Slept

While Americans have been busy Facebooking, sleeping, watching television, and other social media, these corporations have been busy at work, locking in and tidying up their death grip over every aspect of employees' carefully scripted lives. Certainly, rules of work have always shifted, but not at such a rapid pace (Bolles, 2021). The change and pace of rules of work are expected to increase as the COVID-19 pandemic endures.

In the "just f*cking do it" environment, a slim minority are ringing the alarm bells, but like abused children, their cries go unheeded. In the Google employees statement to its leadership, the 600 Google employees (as cited in Elias, 2021a) said that "it [the Google COVID-19 vaccine mandate] normalizes medical intervention compulsion not only for Covid-19 vaccination but for future vaccines and possibly even non-vaccine interventions by extension" ("The mandate dilemma," para. 13).

The non-vaccine interventions by extension include, for example, chipping employees with microchips.

According to Barnhizer and Barnhizer (2019), forcing employees to get microchipped has already raised red flags. As noted by Astor (2017), chipping employees can sound conspiratorial, but it is not because this issue represents the real deal, mentioning some employees have already volunteered to be chipped.

Chips are being used to replace employees' credentials but their usage could expand, providing employers greater control of their workforce (Firfiray, 2018). Wright (2017) noted that chipped employees have been able to "log on to computers, open doors, use the copy machine and purchase food at work instead of using a badge or a credit card" (para. 3). Unfortunately, Cowan and Morell (2021) observed that one of the possible consequences of the COVID-19 pandemic is compulsory microchipping.

If states and private corporations can force vaccination, eventually they will be at the courthouse arguing before the judge to have employees chipped because of company policy. And when employees refuse, they will be terminated for violating company policy. And like the COVID-19 pandemic has shown, employees who refused to get chipped will not be able to claim unemployment because they were terminated for cause (i.e., not getting chipped because it was company policy).

Chapter 26

Social Experience of COVID-19

Geiling (2013) noted that to think of the AIDS epidemic only as a medical phenomenon dismisses the social experience of the era. With COVID-19, the same thing holds, although COVID-19 is a medical occurrence, COVID-19 has swept its social dynamics worldwide. For example, during both the AIDS and COVID-19 outbreaks were two Republicans (and it could have just as well been Democrats), Ronald Reagan, the 40th president of the United States, and Donald Trump, the 45th president of the United States.

Chapter 27

A Joke

Joke exchanges are carried on in deadly earnest, like a verbal duel-mouth-to-mouth combat. Bang, bang: you're (linguistically) dead. —David Crystal

According to Lopez (2016), the Reagan administration's initial exhibited response included treating AIDS as a "joke" (para. 1). Summers (2020) noted that Trump "downplayed," even undermined public health officials, and self-reported that he wanted "to always play it down" (paras. 2-3).

Politicians will be politicians, even in a pandemic. Politicians claim to adhere to the science but ultimately abide by a script (de Waal, 2021). It is like kissing babies in an election year or showing up to a local church, it is all for show. Although following this script is dangerous for society, politicians have become "poll-iticians," the politician who does nothing without consulting poll numbers.

Chapter 28

Misinformation

In life you will face a lot of Circuses.
—William H. McRaven

Like the 1980s, some people took advantage of others, disseminating misinformation. Indeed, misinformation generally follows the broadcast stage of pandemics (S. Taylor, 2021). Bond (2021) reported, for example, that a link to a Facebook story that suggested the COVID-19 vaccine may have been involved with a doctor's demise received much attention in the first quarter of the COVID-19 pandemic. Indeed, fearmongering through print media occurred using similar deceptive means in the 1980s (Geiling, 2013). Fake news, alternative facts, and simply lying is not exclusive to COVID-19 but a part of the social phenomenon of our era.

President Biden (as cited in the White House, 2021) said that "the unvaccinated are responsible for their own choices. But those choices have been fueled by dangerous misinformation on cable TV and social media" (Section 12:33 – 12:45). I agree, misinformation has been and continues to be a problem. What President Biden left out is that the government, including state governments, have added to the erroneous information, especially by being less than candid. Rosenblum & Muirhead (2020) noted that even people in government submit to and use misinformation for political persuasions.

Misinformation in the age of COVID-19 has taken on a new meaning and a new urgency. First social media allows information to be disseminated broadly. And second, with the ability to reach more people, it can reach people quicker than in past generations. According to Rid (2020), the ability to spread disinformation was once a slow and labor-intensive task that has now become fast and a much less labor-intensive effort to spread psychological influence. With a few clicks, misinformation can be extensively shared.

With the overload of information, connecting with people deep and quick minimizes opportunities to get quality facts out concerning COVID-19 and other legitimate information. This is not a partisan issue, there are cooks on both sides of the ideological spectrum, both Democrats and Republicans.

Susarla et al. (2021) noted that absent meaningful regulation of social media, misinformation is likely to increase. Seymour (2020) noted that if social media "confronts us with a string of calamities—addiction, depression, 'fake news,' trolls, online mobs, alt-right subcultures—it is only exploiting and magnifying problems that are already socially pervasive" (p. 11). Taken together, unfortunately, regulation will only push something that is already there underground.

One thing that is clear from all the misinformation that is circulating is that sometimes-well-meaning people could also be spreading information that is less than factual.

The sad truth is that the highest-ranked hold the power of the purse and control the news media. And people consume a lot of news: television, radio, and social media (Giles, 2010). Media, regardless of type, has become so tightly integrated into daily life that people rarely distinguish mediated experience from other segments of their life (Stever et al., 2021).

The new media reality presents a bode ill as there are inherent disconnects in how different generations absorb, disseminate, present, or malign media. In the book, *The Misinformation Age: How False Beliefs Spread*, O'Connor and Weatherall (2019) noted that "if you believe false things about the world, and you make decisions on the basis of those beliefs, then those decisions are unlikely to yield the outcomes you expect and desire" (p. 5). Unfortunately, *without the ability to obtain the expectations and desires of life, it creates a world where people seek instant gratification, a refuge from so many disappointments and regrets*. Accordingly, false beliefs about the world essentially allow manipulation artists, both the government facilitators or private actors, to cast their misinformation to which people act.

For example, in Governor Hochul's eagerness to dismiss people's religious beliefs as ungodly, she also trashed social media. Governor Hochul failed to understand by trashing social media, she also dismissed a generation of people who grew up on social media. Or perhaps, Governor Hochul does not care.

Chapter 29

Fake News

*...the passage of time, combined with new
experience and research, makes yesterday's
'facts' today's myths, superstitions and
falsehoods. — Dick Gregory*

According to Susarla et al. (2021), fake news has reached a new peak, including costing countless lives through the COVID-19 pandemic.

Fake news is often sensational, designed to reach people's emotions with false information (Greifeneder et al., 2020), which is why propaganda is so dangerous. Fake news appears under the guise of legitimate news (Brotherton, 2020). Fake news is not about news outlets getting information incorrect (Brotherton, 2020), which is common from time to time. Fake news is about disseminating untruths, propaganda.

Propaganda, like other misinformation, according to Susarla et al. (2021), "is not the result of innocent misunderstanding. It's the product of specific campaigns to advance a political or ideological agenda." (Propaganda by another name," para. 1). Thus it is also important to understand that even legitimate news sources "serve, and propagandize on behalf of, the powerful societal interests that control and finance them" (Herman & Chomsky, 2011, p. 8). Hence, propaganda is about capitalizing on the psychology of the misinformed.

Once unleashed, propaganda can get out of hand. Propaganda supplants one's ability to think, replacing it with "impulses, habits, and emotions" (Bernays, 2004, p. 73). Propaganda, no matter what side it comes from, "when supported by the educated class and when no deviation is permitted from it, can have a big effect" (Chomsky, 2011, p. 13). It is all about the hearts and minds. Propaganda is like a beautiful poison with intoxicating effects, but devastating consequences. Hence, Dick (1995) noted that defining what is real is both critical and essential.

What is real is this: Governmental public policy has allowed more people to encounter COVID-19 than what was desired to end the pandemic, and this has allowed businesses and special interests, who are even less equipped to address COVID-19 to run roughshod over its employee all for a dollar. This ill-advised public policy has been disastrous for the American people. Such policies have caused thousands of hours of unnecessary frustration at airline terminals (Chokshi & Murphy, 2021) and American businesses, for example (Gelles & Goldberg, 2021). Unnecessary closures. And ultimately unnecessary deaths.

Chapter 30

National Coordination

Inequality can have a bad downside, but equality, for its part, sure does get in the way of coordination. —Mary Douglas

According to Curran and Jaffe (2011), by the mid-1980s, AIDS had become a nationally coordinated effort. However, to date, the COVID-19 response is still being piecemealed at the state level with varying results. The lack of national coordination includes the lack of COVID-19 testing.

Parmet (2022) noted that states are unable to address these national issues because they cross many different jurisdictions and national coordination is appropriate under pandemic and other national issues. While some people always look to national coordination, states throughout the United States' history have come and worked on issues of importance.

Unfortunately, E. Goldberg et al. (2022) reported that some employees are getting all the COVID-19 tests they need from their companies, such as Google. This is part of the lack of national coordination by the federal government. Compare this to all the Americans standing in lines to be tested. The lack of coordination has revealed another disparity in the American caste system. Corporations are not offering COVID-19 tests for altruistic purposes, every dollar is documented and tracked by their accountants for either reimbursement or tax incentives from the same federal government that has, in part, created such disparity. Ultimately, if you work for these wealthy companies, you will be taken care of while those not working for Google or any of these multinationals are left standing out in the cold, literally.

Chapter 31

Shame and Humiliation

Humiliation is more dangerous than
plutonium. —Robert W. Fuller

Beyond what is known as 'COVID shame,' a shame of developing or being related to someone who had caught COVID-19, people are dealing with all sorts of shame from the pandemic (Paul, 2021, para. 2). Just like some experienced COVID shame, the unvaccinated have been shamed too.

The unvaccinated, unfortunately, contend with the same burdens as those who received the "AIDS labeling," the name-calling such as the "gay plague," the discrimination, and the strained relationships (J. W. Curran & Jaffe, 2011, p. 65). Fetters (2020) noted that people are losing friends over COVID-19, too. Breen (2021) reported that 1 out of 7 people stopped being friends with others over their COVID-19 vaccination status. If we were watching a movie, this would represent a rerun using a film noir effect with no dénouement.

A film noir effect depicts alienation and deception, and in the COVID-19 era, deceit and hostility have run rampant. Untangling the threads of the damage that has resulted from the COVID-19 pandemic will occur over many years. Anthropologists, psychologists, and psychiatrists will spend many years unpacking the shame and humiliation that has followed in the era of COVID-19. After all, society is still reeling from the fallout of the AIDS epidemic: the missed opportunities, the slow progress to corrected social ills, and the inability to control the effects of the AIDS epidemic.

Chapter 32

No Proof No Service Policies

Restaurant servers, bartenders and ticket agents become the frontline enforcers for vaccination rules. —Associated Press

Imagine arriving at your favorite restaurant and being asked to produce a copy of your AIDS status or risk being denied service. Hupka (2021) noted that a few states established a reopening structure that focuses on compelling COVID-19 vaccination proof for certain events. As such, individuals and organizations appear to have been given a blank check to discriminate, openly.

With the ability to require proof of vaccination, the paper proof will become antiquated and unusable as proof. Somethings have an insidious way off starting voluntarily and then, when people become comfortable with it, such as digital vaccination cards, it becomes the de facto, required standard.

Take, for example, driver's licenses. In 2005, under the Real ID Act, the federal government required states to standardize driver's licenses nationwide. Many states objected, but the federal government made it clear that the current driver's licenses would not be accepted for boarding aircraft or entering federal facilities. Eventually, every state capitulated, even the most ardent objectors. Hence, driver's licenses became national ID cards.

Ingram (2022) reported that a national push for a digital vaccination card is underway. Indeed, a worldwide digital vaccination card is the ultimate goal (World Health Organization (WHO), 2021a). The digital vaccination card is known as the "SMART Health Card," eliminating the need for the paper card distributed by the CDC (Ingram, 2022, para. 2).

Chapter 33

The People's Assessment

The difficulty is that the history of medicine
includes enough moral outrages, good-faith
errors, and unanticipated calamities to justify
critical questioning. —Alex de Waal

Brown (2009) wrote, discussing AIDS, "we have not been told the truth about this biological threat" (p. 142), noting the upheaval presented worldwide proportion. Doka (2014) opined that AIDS is just one of many pathogens and because of people's fears and irrational responses, such fears and responses prevented society's ability to halt its transmission.

If fear and irrationality stunted society's ability to halt AIDS transmission, people's fears and irrational responses to COVID-19 have provided equal opportunity to stop COVID-19's transmission. Concerning COVID-19, reasons for not taking the vaccine include "not trusting the vaccine and not trusting the government" (King et al., 2021; University of Pittsburgh Medical Center (UPMC), 2021, para. 9). The study found that vaccine hesitancy was high among respondents who hold a doctoral degree (King et al., 2021). The world's most well-educated and well-trained individuals on earth have declined vaccination.

At the time of the reporting, about 60 million Americans continue to be unvaccinated (Elias, 2021a). As of Christmas 2021, Healy et al. (2021) reported that about 39 million Americans remain unvaccinated, noting that "skepticism and wariness... [seem to be similar to] an article of faith" (para. 3). Still, many organizations and the news media would have the unvaccinated believe something is wrong with them. People, however, worldwide view vaccines with skepticism, not just Americans (Brotherton, 2015). Many countries hold a storied past, overrun with examples of why these concerns are valid.

Chapter 34

The Final Word

The COVID-19 pandemic like any other medical event or natural disaster holds a social component. One of COVID-19's social components is the mass termination of employees. Organizations are making judgment calls about employee separation (Arnow-Richman, 2021). Employees were not required to be terminated, organizations, on their own accord, decided to implement policies that, at first blush, appear to try to move the economy in a positive direction, but when looking under the hood, these organizational policies lacked basic humanity and were focused on their bottom line.

Dumping employees on this large scale is not only abrasive to an organization's optics but also not good for society because mass termination from COVID-19 strains an already strained system with such organizational practices.

The response from organizations to COVID-19 came in the form of copying and pasting, narrow framing organizational objectives, and wasting resources because organizations switched between multiple options without properly weighing the risks to organizations and their people. When organizations fail to have a people strategy, when lean times or crisis events come, such organizations overly rely on sledgehammer tactics when a scalpel would work. Failure to have a people strategy also leaves no room for empathy when events such as COVID-19 arise.

One of the benefits of a people strategy is that it allows organizations to develop humanity into their policies and procedures, and a people strategy keeps organizations consistent with how they address issues with employment, especially when society is moving toward healthier workplaces through the United Nations' SDGs. When organizations fail to invest in their people, they also fail to enable maximum corporate objectives. Altman (2021) noted that when people strategies are lacking, organizations remove opportunities to course correct, especially how employees feel.

Organizations have had much time, especially over the last two decades, to learn how to address upheaval and uncertainty. Uncertainty, according to Buckley (2021), represents a workplace standard. Gelles and Goldberg (2021) that CEOs care a lot about certainty. But in the COVID-19 pandemic, CEOs' penchant for certainty has contributed to so much uncertainty. And as such, corporations have depleted their organizational capital, not maximizing their resources to achieve the full benefit of their organizations.

Organizations based on rulers and the ruled will find it hard to keep pace with corporations that have a people strategy that values the human resource.

References

12 News. (2019, June 6). *Allied Universal employees claim cover-up after video shows Segway accident.* Youtube. https://www.youtube.com/watch?v=qd8eoimLDZ4

Aarssen, C. (2019). *The clutter connection: How your personality type determines why you organize the way you do.* Blackstone Publishing.

ABC 4 Utah. (2021, December 2). *Vaccine mandate paused, healthcare workers react.* YouTube. https://www.youtube.com/watch?v=B4zJzjCiYww

Acemoglu, D., & Robinson, J. A. (2012). *Why nations fail: The origins of power, prosperity, and poverty* (1st ed.). Currency.

AFL-CIO, American Apparel & Footwear Association, Fontheim International, & Human Rights Watch. (2021, October 29). *Letter to Biden Administration: Use G20 to advance social protection.* https://www.hrw.org/news/2021/10/29/letter-biden-administration-use-g20-advance-social-protection

Albeck-Ripka, L. (2022, January 4). *A federal judge blocks the Defense Dept. from punishing Navy forces who refuse the vaccine.* The New York Times. https://www.nytimes.com/2022/01/04/us/lawsuit-us-troops-vaccine-exemption.html

Allport, G. W., (with Clark, K., & (with Pettigrew, T. (1979). *The nature of prejudice: 25th-anniversary edition* (Unabridged). Basic Books.

Altman, J. (2021). *People strategy: How to invest in people and make culture your competitive advantage* (1st ed.). John Wiley & Sons.

Altschuler, G. C. (2022, January 9). *How to hold unvaccinated Americans accountable.* The Hill. https://thehill.com/opinion/finance/588892-how-to-hold-unvaccinated-americans-accountable

Amanpour and Company. (2021, November 30). *"Herd immunity is off the table" says infectious disease specialist | Amanpour and Company.* YouTube. https://www.youtube.com/watch?v=uoZE9d1LJfg&t=616s

Amen, D. G. (2021). *Your brain is always listening: Tame the hidden dragons that control your happiness, habits, and hang-ups.* Tyndale Momentum.

American Psychiatric Association. (2013). *Diagnostic and statistical manual of mental disorders* (5th ed.). https://doi.org/10.1176/appi.books.9780890425596

American RadioWorks. (1964, August 22). *Fannie Lou Hamer (1917-1977): Testimony Before the Credentials Committee, Democratic National Convention.* Apmreports.Org. https://americanradioworks.publicradio.org/features/sayitplain/flhamer.html

Amnesty International. (2021, November 8). *Americas: Human rights are essential for a renewal of the region.* Amnesty.Org. https://www.amnesty.org/en/latest/news/2021/11/americas-human-rights-essential-renewal-region/

Andrews, M. (2021, November 3). *Families could be denied death benefits if their unvaccinated loved one dies.* Cable News Network (CNN). https://www.cnn.com/2021/11/03/health/unvaccinated-death-benefits-khn-partner/index.html

Anthes, E., & Weiland, N. (2021, December 29). *As Omicron spreads, officials ponder what it means to be 'fully vaccinated.'* The New York Times. https://www.nytimes.com/2021/12/29/health/covid-vaccinations-boosters.html

Aravindan, A., & Lin, C. (2021, July 23). *Vaccinated people make up 75% of recent COVID-19 cases in Singapore, but few fall ill.* Reuters. https://www.reuters.com/world/asia-pacific/vaccinated-people-singapore-make-up-three-quarters-recent-covid-19-cases-2021-07-23/

Arieti, S. (1972). *The will to be human.* Quadrangle Books.

Armstrong, S., & Mitchell, B. (2019). *The essential HR handbook: A quick and handy resource for any manager or HR professional* (10th Anniversary). Career Press.

Arnold, J., Coyne, I., Randall, R., & Patterson, F. (2020). *Work psychology* (7th ed.). Pearson Education.

Arnow-Richman, R. (2021). Temporary termination: Layoff law blueprint for the COVID era. *Washington University Journal of Law & Policy, 64,* 1–30.

Ashford, G. (2021, November 14). *Dozens of N.Y.C. sanitation workers were suspended during an inquiry into the use of fake vaccine cards.* New York Times. https://www.nytimes.com/live/2021/11/14/world/covid-vaccine-boosters-mandate#sanitation-workers-fake-vaccine-cards

Ashton, J. (2021). *The new normal: A roadmap to resilience in the Pandemic Era* (1st ed.). William Morrow.

Associated Press. (2021, October 11). *Texas Gov. Greg Abbott orders a ban on all COVID-19 vaccine mandates in the state.* National Public Radio (NPR). https://www.npr.org/2021/10/11/1045142578/texas-governor-greg-abbott-ban-covid-vaccine-mandates

Astor, M. (2017, July 25). *Microchip implants for employees? One company says yes.* The New York Times. https://www.nytimes.com/2017/07/25/technology/microchips-wisconsin-company-employees.html

Atlas, S. W. (2021). *A plague upon our house: My fight at the Trump White House to stop COVID from destroying America.* Bombardier Books.

Avery, D. R., & Ruggs, E. N. (2020, July 14). *Confronting the uncomfortable reality of workplace discrimination.* MIT Sloan Management Review. https://sloanreview.mit.edu/article/confronting-the-uncomfortable-reality-of-workplace-discrimination/

Babiak, P., & Hare, R. D. (2009). *Snakes in suits: When psychopaths go to work.* HarperCollins.

Bachmann, H., Beattie, K., Stefanini, P., & Welchman, T. (2021, September 23). *Banking on the 'soft stuff.'* Mckinsey & Company. https://www.mckinsey.com/business-functions/transformation/our-insights/banking-on-the-soft-stuff

Bade, R., Daniels, E., Lizza, R., & Palmeri, T. (2021, December 1). *Politico playbook: Scoop: Conservatives plot government shutdown over vaccine mandate.* Politico. https://www.politico.com/newsletters/playbook/2021/12/01/scoop-conservatives-plot-government-shutdown-over-vaccine-mandate-495273?nname=playbook&nid=0000014f-1646-d88f-a1cf-5f46b7bd0000&nrid=49b86ef8-991f-4f21-8c07-c9f77e68b398&nlid=630318

Baker, D. (2016). *Rigged: How globalization and the rules of the modern economy were structured to make the rich richer* (1st ed.). Center for Economic and Policy Research.

Balch, B. (2021, October 26). *The cost of being unvaccinated is rising — will people be willing to pay the price?* Association of American Medical Colleges. https://www.aamc.org/news-insights/cost-being-unvaccinated-rising-will-people-be-willing-pay-price

Banaji, M. R., & Greenwald, A. G. (2013). *Blindspot: Hidden biases of good people* (1st ed.). Delacorte Press.

Bank, S. A., Blair, M. M., Bloch, R. H., Crane, D. A., Hennessey, J. L., Hilt, E., Levy, J., Lichtenstein, N., Mehrotra, A. K., Pollman, E., Wallis, J. J., & Winkler, A. (2017). *Corporations and American Democracy* (N. R. Lamoreaux & W. J. Novak (Eds.)). Harvard University Press.

Barnhizer, D., & Barnhizer, D. D. (2019). *The artificial intelligence contagion: Can democracy withstand the imminent transformation of work, wealth and the social order?* Skyboat Media.

Barone, M. (2004). *Hard America, soft America: Competition vs. coddling and the battle for the nation's future.* Crown Forum.

Barrabi, T. (2021, December 8). *Senate votes to repeal Biden federal vaccine mandate for businesses.* Fox Business. https://www.foxbusiness.com/politics/senate-votes-repeal-biden-federal-vaccine-mandate-businesses

Barrero, J. M., Bloom, N., & Davis, S. J. (2022, January 25). *Why companies aren't cutting back on office space.* Harvard Business Review. https://hbr.org/2022/01/why-companies-arent-cutting-back-on-office-space

Barry, J. J., Christiano, A., & Neimand, A. (2021, September 24). *Half of unvaccinated workers say they'd rather quit than get a shot – but real-world data suggest few are following through.* The Conversation. https://theconversation.com/half-of-unvaccinated-workers-say-theyd-rather-quit-than-get-a-shot-but-real-world-data-suggest-few-are-following-through-168447

Basford, T., & Schaninger, B. (2016, April 11). *The four building blocks of change.* McKinsey Quarterly. https://www.mckinsey.com/business-functions/organization/our-insights/the-four-building-blocks--of-change

Baumeister, R. F., & Tierney, J. (2011). *Willpower: Rediscovering the greatest human strength* (1st ed.). Penguin Books.

Beals, M. (2021, December 20). *New Zealand links death to Pfizer COVID vaccine: "it remains safer to be vaccinated."* The Hill. https://thehill.com/policy/healthcare/586516-new-zealand-links-26-year-olds-death-to-pfizer-covid-vaccine

Becker, E., & Keen, S. (2007). *The denial of death* (1st ed.). Free Press.

Bell Hooks. (2014). *Teaching to transgress: Education as the practice of freedom* (1st ed.). Routledge.

Benoit, W. L. (1997). Image repair discourse and crisis communication. *Public Relations Review, 23*(2), 177–186. https://doi.org/10.1016/S0363-8111(97)90023-0

Berenson, A. (2021). *Pandemia: How coronavirus hysteria took over our government, rights, and lives.* Regnery Publishing.

Bergal, J. (2021, September 16). *Fake vaccine card sales have skyrocketed since Biden mandate.* Pew Charitable Trusts. https://www.pewtrusts.org/en/research-and-analysis/blogs/stateline/2021/09/16/fake-vaccine-card-sales-have-skyrocketed-since-biden-mandate

Bergstrom, C. T., & West, J. D. (2020). *Calling bullshit: The art of skepticism in a data-driven world.* Random House.

Bernanke, B. S. (2015). *The courage to act: A memoir of a crisis and its aftermath* (Illustrated). W. W. Norton & Company.

Bernays, E., & (with Miller, M. C. (2004). *Propaganda.* Ig Publishing.

Bernhard, M. (2021, December 15). *What if there's no such thing as closure?* The New York Times Magazine. https://www.nytimes.com/2021/12/15/magazine/grieving-loss-closure.html

Better Business Bureaus (BBB). (n.d.). *Customer reviews for Allied Universal.* https://www.bbb.org/us/pa/conshohocken/profile/security-guards/allied-universal-0241-3802345/customer-reviews

Bhanot, D., Singh, T., Verma, S. K., & Sharad, S. (2021). Stigma and discrimination during COVID-19 pandemic. *Frontiers in Public Health, 8.* https://doi.org/10.3389/fpubh.2020.577018

Bhanot, S. (2020, May 5). *You're stronger than your quarantine fatigue.* New York Times. https://www.nytimes.com/2020/05/05/opinion/coronavirus-quarantine-fatigue.html

Bhaskar, M. (2021). *Human frontiers: The future of big ideas in an age of small thinking.* MIT Press.

Biden, Joseph Robinette, J. (2021, September 9). *Remarks by President Biden on fighting the COVID-19 Pandemic*. The White House. https://www.whitehouse.gov/briefing-room/speeches-remarks/2021/09/09/remarks-by-president-biden-on-fighting-the-covid-19-pandemic-3/

Biden, J. R. J. (2021, December 9). *Remarks by President Biden at the Summit for Democracy opening session*. White House. https://www.whitehouse.gov/briefing-room/speeches-remarks/2021/12/09/remarks-by-president-biden-at-the-summit-for-democracy-opening-session/

Birkel, D. J., & Miller, S. J. (1998). *Career bounce-back: The professionals in transition guide to recovery and reemployment*. American Management Association. https://archive.org/details/careerbounceback00jdam

Black, C. H. (1990). *Black's law dictionary* (6th ed.). West Group.

Blackmon, D. A. (2008). *Slavery by another name: The re-enslavement of Black Americans from the Civil War to World War II* (Reprint). Anchor.

Blair, R. J. R. (2018). Traits of empathy and anger: Implications for psychopathy and other disorders associated with aggression. *Philosophical Transactions of the Royal Society B: Biological Sciences, 373*(1744), 20170155. https://doi.org/10.1098/rstb.2017.0155

Blakemore, E. (2018, July 26). *How the US Ended up with warehouses full of "Government Cheese."* History. https://www.history.com/news/government-cheese-dairy-farmers-reagan

Bolles, G. A. (2021). *The next rules of work: The mindset, skillset and toolset to lead your organization through uncertainty* (1st ed.). Kogan Page.

Bollinger, R., & Ray, S. (2021, October 5). *COVID variants: What you should know*. Johns Hopkins Medicine. https://www.hopkinsmedicine.org/health/conditions-and-diseases/coronavirus/a-new-strain-of-coronavirus-what-you-should-know

Bonanno, G. A. (2021). *The end of trauma: How the new science of resilience is changing how we think about PTSD*. Basic Books.

Bond, S. (2021, August 21). *Facebook's most viewed article in early 2021 raised doubt about COVID vaccine*. National Public Radio (NPR).

https://www.npr.org/2021/08/21/1030038616/facebooks-most-viewed-article-in-early-2021-raised-doubt-about-covid-vaccine

Boss, P. (2021). *The myth of closure: Ambiguous loss in a time of pandemic and change.* W. W. Norton & Company.

Bowler, K. (2021). *No cure for being human: (And other truths I need to hear).* Random House.

Boyes, A. (2015). *The anxiety toolkit: Strategies for fine-tuning your mind and moving past your stuck points.* Tarcher Perigee.

Brackett, A. G., & Sullivan, D. P. (2022). *Employer obligations in administering COVID-19 vaccine mandates when facing religious exemption requests.* Reuters. https://www.reuters.com/legal/litigation/employer-obligations-administering-covid-19-vaccine-mandates-when-facing-2022-01-18/

Bradshaw, J. (2010). *Healing the shame that binds you.* Health Communications.

Breeden, A. (2022, January 5). *Macron under fire after arguing France should make life miserable for the unvaccinated.* The New York Times. https://www.nytimes.com/2022/01/05/world/macron-france-life-miserable-unvaccinated.html

Breen, K. (2021, September 16). *1 in 7 people ended friendships over COVID-19 vaccine stance, survey finds.* Today. https://www.today.com/health/1-7-people-have-ended-friendships-over-covid-19-vaccine-t231279

Bremen, J. M., Ganu, S., Sung, A., & Wurtzel, M. (2021, September 2). *Human capital is the key to a successful ESG strategy.* World Economic Forum. https://www.weforum.org/agenda/2021/09/human-capital-is-the-key-to-a-successful-esg-strategy/

British Broadcasting Corporation (BBC). (2022a, January 4). *Covid: French uproar as Macron vows to "piss off" unvaccinated.* https://www.bbc.com/news/world-europe-59873833

British Broadcasting Corporation (BBC). (2022b, January 17). *Credit Suisse boss Horta-Osorio resigns over Covid breaches.* https://www.bbc.com/news/business-60019735

Brooks, D. (2011). *The social animal: The hidden sources of love, character, and achievement.* Random House.

Brooks, D. (2022, January 13). *America is falling apart at the seams.* The New York Times. https://www.nytimes.com/2022/01/13/opinion/america-falling-apart.html

Brooks, K. J. (2021, December 1). *Moderna's CEO says current COVID-19 vaccines likely won't work as well against Omicron.* CBS News. https://www.cbsnews.com/news/covid-omicron-variant-vaccine-moderna/

Brotherton, R. (2015). *Suspicious minds: Why we believe conspiracy theories* (1st ed.). Bloomsbury Sigma.

Brotherton, R. (2020). *Bad news: Why we fall for fake news* (1st ed.). Bloomsbury Sigma.

Brown, B. (2013). *The power of vulnerability: Teachings on authenticity, connection and courage* (1st ed.). Sounds True.

Brown, M. (2020). *I don't agree: Why we can't stop fighting – and how to get great stuff done despite our differences.* Harriman House.

Brown, T. (2009). *Black lies, white lies: The truth according to Tony Brown.* Perennial.

Brown, K. V. (2021, December 5). *What's the difference between a mutation and a strain?* Bloomberg. https://www.bloomberg.com/news/newsletters/2021-12-05/coronavirus-daily-is-a-virus-mutation-omicron-different-from-a-strain

Brunnermeier, M. (2021). *The resilient society* (1st ed.). Endeavor Literary Press.

BST Holdings v. OSHA 21-60845, (2021).

Buckley, P. (2021). *Change on the run: 44 ways to survive workplace uncertainty.* Page Two.

Bumbaca, C. (2021, December 26). *Antonio Brown, returning for Buccaneers after fake vaccine card, can still earn $1 million in incentives.* USA Today. https://www.usatoday.com/story/sports/nfl/buccaneers/2021/12/26/buccaneers-antonio-brown-contract-incentives/9018567002/

Burgo, J. (2018). *Shame: Free yourself, find joy, and build true self-esteem.* Brilliance Audio.

Cable, D. M. (2019). *Alive at work: The neuroscience of helping your people love what they do*. Harvard Business Review Press.

Cable News Network (CNN). (2006, May 4). *Study: Geography Greek to young Americans*. CNN.Com. http://edition.cnn.com/2006/EDUCATION/05/02/geog.test/index.html

Cable News Network (CNN). (2021, December 2). *The reason we're becoming more extreme*. YouTube. https://www.youtube.com/watch?v=t_G240I5zF8&t=205s

Cameron, J. (1997). *Titanic*. Twentieth Century Fox.

Campbell, C. (2012). *Scapegoat: A history of blaming other people*. ABRAMS Press.

Campos, S. (2021, December 17). *CDC Director Dr. Walensky says any vaccine is better than none in recommending J&J's Covid shots*. CNBC. https://www.cnbc.com/2021/12/17/cdc-director-says-any-vaccine-is-better-than-none-in-recommending-jj-covid-shots.html

Cann, O. (2015, September 23). *How can the development goals be achieved?* World Economic Forum. https://www.weforum.org/agenda/2015/09/how-achievable-are-the-sustainable-development-goals/

Cappelli, P. (2021). *The future of the office: Work from home, remote work, and the hard choices we all face*. Wharton School Press.

Carse, J. P. (2011). *Finite and infinite games*. Free Press.

Carson, C. (Ed.). (2001). *The autobiography of Martin Luther King, Jr.* Grand Central Publishing.

Cartaya, M., & Elamroussi, A. (2021, December 23). *North Carolina police chief placed on unpaid leave for telling officers about "clinic" to obtain Covid-19 vaccination cards without getting the shots*. Cable News Network (CNN). https://www.cnn.com/2021/12/23/us/north-carolina-police-chief-disciplined-vaccine-fraud/index.html

Casselman, B. (2022, January 4). *More workers quit than ever as U.S. job openings remain near a record*. The New York Times. https://www.nytimes.com/2022/01/04/business/economy/job-openings-coronavirus.html

Cave, D. (2021, August 20). *Australia is betting on remote quarantine.*

Here's what I learned on the inside. The New York Times. https://www.nytimes.com/2021/08/20/world/australia/howard-springs-quarantine.html

Chamberlain, A., & Zhao, D. (2019, August 19). *The key to happy customers? Happy employees.* Harvard Business Review. https://hbr.org/2019/08/the-key-to-happy-customers-happy-employees

Chatterjee, D. (2021, December 1). *Business unusual: The pandemic forces a social reset.* MIT Salon Management Review. https://sloanreview.mit.edu/article/business-unusual-the-pandemic-forces-a-social-reset/

Chemaitelly, H., Tang, P., Hasan, M. R., AlMukdad, S., Yassine, H. M., Benslimane, F. M., Al Khatib, H. A., Coyle, P., Ayoub, H. H., Al Kanaani, Z., Al Kuwari, E., Jeremijenko, A., Kaleeckal, A. H., Latif, A. N., Shaik, R. M., Abdul Rahim, H. F., Nasrallah, G. K., Al Kuwari, M. G., Al Romaihi, H. E., ... Abu-Raddad, L. J. (2021). Waning of BNT162b2 vaccine protection against SARS-CoV-2 infection in Qatar. *New England Journal of Medicine, 385*(24), e83. https://doi.org/10.1056/NEJMoa2114114

Chen, S. (2021, March 13). *Wealthy people are taking COVID-19 vaccines allotted for others.* Axios. https://www.axios.com/covid-vaccine-wealthy-people-fd47f852-0e92-4581-aaf2-e0690877116a.html

Cheng, A. (2021, December 18). *Boeing drops vaccine mandate for U.S. workers, joining Amtrak and other major federal contractors.* The Washington Post. https://www.washingtonpost.com/nation/2021/12/18/boeing-vaccine-mandate-lawsuit/

Choi, I., & Cha, O. (2019). Cross-cultural examination of the false consensus effect. *Frontiers in Psychology, 10.* https://doi.org/10.3389/fpsyg.2019.02747

Chokshi, N., & Murphy, H. (2021, December 30). *Air travel is no holiday as Covid and storms cancel flights.* The New York Times. https://www.nytimes.com/2021/12/30/business/flights-cancelled.html

Chomsky, N. (2011). *Media control: The spectacular achievements of propaganda* (2nd ed.). Seven Stories Press.

Chomsky, N. (2015). *What kind of creatures are we?* Columbia University Press.

Chopra, D. (2021). Episode 1a: Meditation: Self-acceptance. In *Deepak Chopra's mind body zone: Living outside the box*. Audible Original. https://www.audible.com/pd/Deepak-Chopras-Mind-Body-Zone-Living-Outside-the-Box-Podcast/episodes/B099Y3Z9VP?ref=a_pd_Deepak_c3_episodes_view_all&pf_rd_p=625c212d-b95a-47db-8d56-d35a359de6e9&pf_rd_r=06NFEFH5CCSX15DW4H1N

Christakis, N. A. (2020). *Apollo's Arrow: The profound and enduring impact of coronavirus on the way we live* (1st ed.). Little, Brown Spark.

Chua, A. (2018). *Political tribes: Group instinct and the fate of nations*. Penguin Books.

Chuck, E. (2021, December 16). *Growing number of companies suspend vaccine mandates, including hospitals and Amtrak*. NBCNews.Com. https://www.nbcnews.com/news/us-news/companies-suspend-vaccine-mandates-hospitals-amtrak-rcna8903

Clark, T. R. (2020). *The 4 stages of psychological safety: Defining the path to inclusion and innovation*. Berrett-Koehler Publishers.

Clawson, J. G. (1986). *A leader's guide to why people behave the way they do. Darden Case No. UVA-OB-0744*. Darden Business Publishing. https://ssrn.com/abstract=911080

Coe, E., Cordina, J., Enomoto, K., & Stueland, J. (2021, June 15). *Returning to work: Keys to a psychologically safer workplace*. Mckinsey. https://www.mckinsey.com/industries/healthcare-systems-and-services/our-insights/returning-to-work-keys-to-a-psychologically-safer-workplace

Cohen, A. (2021, June 16). *As U.S. returns to the office, Europe has tips on what to do—and not do*. Bloomberg. https://www.bloomberg.com/news/articles/2021-06-16/tips-from-european-bosses-for-a-u-s-headed-back-to-the-office-as-covid-recedes

Cohn, A. (2019, August 29). *'Mental rigidity' at the root of intense political partisanship on both left and right – study*. University of Cambridge. https://www.cam.ac.uk/research/news/mental-rigidity-at-the-root-of-intense-political-partisanship-on-both-left-and-right-study

Collier, P. (2018). *The future of capitalism: Facing the new anxieties*. Harper.

Collins, J., & Hansen, M. T. (2011). *Great by choice: Uncertainty, chaos, and luck--Why some thrive despite them all.* HarperCollins.

Collinson, S. (2021, December 30). *Biden administration signals pandemic strategy shift in the face of Omicron.* Cable News Network (CNN). https://www.cnn.com/2021/12/30/politics/biden-administration-shifting-covid-guidance/index.html

Comen, E. (2019, October 15). *Is your money safe? These states are getting hit hardest by the pension crisis.* USA Today. https://www.usatoday.com/story/money/2019/10/15/every-states-pension-crisis-ranked/40302439/

Cooper, A. (2021, December 6). *New York to mandate Covid vaccines for all private sector workers.* Cable News Network (CNN). https://www.cnn.com/2021/12/06/business/new-york-vaccine-mandate/index.html

Coser, L. A. (1974). *Greedy institutions: Patterns of undivided commitment.* Free Press.

County of Butler, at al. v. Thomas W. Wolf at al. No: 2:20-cv-677, (2020).

Cowan, T. S., & Morell, S. F. (2021). *The truth about contagion: Exploring theories of how disease spreads.* Skyhorse.

Crawford, M. B. (2015). *The world beyond your head: On becoming an individual in an age of distraction.* Farrar, Straus and Giroux.

Crouse, L., Ferguson, K., & Holzknecht, E. (2021, January 23). *Grieving our old normal.* The New York Times. https://www.nytimes.com/2021/12/23/opinion/covid-pandemic-grief.html?searchResultPosition=9

Curran, J. W., & Jaffe, H. W. (2011). AIDS: the early years and CDC's response. *Morbidity and Mortality Weekly Report (MMWR), 60*(04), 64–69.

Curran, L. (2019). *101 trauma-informed interventions: Activities, exercises and assignments to move the client and therapy forward.* PESI Publishing & Media.

Dalai Lama. (2009). *The art of happiness, 10th anniversary edition: A handbook for living.* Riverhead Books.

Dalton, D. (2013). *Power over people: Classical and modern political theory.* Great Courses.

Dasic, D. (2021). *A just society: The world after neoliberalism* (2nd ed.). BGD Solutions.

David, J. E. (2021a, November 5). *The growing link between vaccine mandates and open jobs.* Yahoo Finance. https://finance.yahoo.com/news/the-unlikely-link-between-vaccine-mandate-and-jobs-morning-brief-090610750.html

David, J. E. (2021b, December 29). *Omicron prompts rethink of vaccine impact, COVID-19 mandates: Morning brief.* Yahoo Finance. https://news.yahoo.com/omicron-is-forcing-a-necessary-rethink-of-vaccine-passports-morning-brief-100808464.html

Day, G. S., & Schoemaker, P. J. H. (2019). *See sooner, act faster: How vigilant leaders thrive in an era of digital turbulence.* MIT Press.

de Becker, G. (1997). *The gift of fear: Survival signals that protect us from violence.* Author.

de Vries, M. F. R. K. (2016, April 8). *Seven signs of the greed syndrome.* Insead Knowledge. https://knowledge.insead.edu/blog/insead-blog/seven-signs-of-the-greed-syndrome-4624

de Waal, A. (2021). *New pandemics, old politics: Two hundred years of war on disease and its alternatives* (1st ed.). Wiley.

DeChalus, C., Leonard, K., Rojas, W., & Hall, M. (2021, December 13). *As the pandemic raged, at least 75 lawmakers bought and sold stock in companies that make COVID-19 vaccines, treatments, and tests.* Insider. https://www.businessinsider.com/lawmakers-bought-sold-covid-19-related-stocks-during-pandemic-2021-12

Delavega, E. (2021, September 14). *Poverty got worse in 2020 as many low-wage workers took the brunt of the economic blows.* The Conversation. https://theconversation.com/poverty-got-worse-in-2020-as-many-low-wage-workers-took-the-brunt-of-the-economic-blows-167884

Deloitte. (2021, May 25). *Fixing the plane in flight: Leaders can lean on HR technology to meet the approaching return-to-office challenge.* https://www2.deloitte.com/us/en/blog/human-capital-blog/2021/leaders-lean-on-technology-to-meet-return-to-work-challenges.html

Deming, W. E., & Cahill, K. E. (2018). *The new economics for industry, government, education* (3rd ed.). MIT Press.

Dershowitz, A. (2021). *The case for vaccine mandates.* Hot Books.

Detert, J. R. (2018, November 27). *Speak out successfully*. Harvard Business Review. https://hbr.org/podcast/2018/11/speak-out-successfully

Diaz, J. (2021, June 8). *Fake COVID vaccine cards are being sold online. Using one is a crime*. National Public Radio (NPR). https://www.npr.org/2021/06/08/1004264531/fake-covid-vaccine-cards-keep-getting-sold-online-using-one-is-a-crime

Dick, P. K., & (with Sutin, L. (1995). *The shifting realities of Philip K. Dick: Selected literature and philosophical writings* (L. Sutin (Ed.)). Vintage Books.

Didion, J. (2020). *The year of magical thinking*. Audible Originals.

DiGangi, J. (2021, November 16). *The thing no one told you about your emotional pain*. Psychology Today. https://www.psychologytoday.com/us/blog/reasonable-sanity/202111/the-thing-no-one-told-you-about-your-emotional-pain

Dimsdale, J. E. (2021). *Dark persuasion: A history of brainwashing from Pavlov to social media*. Yale University Press.

District of Columbia Department of Insurance - Securities & Banking. (2021). *Warning signs of a COVID vaccination card scam*.

Dodsworth, L. (2021). *A state of fear: How the UK government weaponized fear during the Covid-19 pandemic* (1st ed.). Pinter & Martin.

Doka, K. J. (2014). *AIDS, fear and society: Challenging the dreaded disease* (1st ed.). Routledge.

Dorrian, P. (2021, September 23). *Allied Universal workers end wage, race bias lawsuit for $30,000*. Bloomberg Law. https://news.bloomberglaw.com/daily-labor-report/allied-universal-workers-end-wage-race-bias-lawsuit-for-30-000

Dostoevsky, F. (2021). *The complete works of Fyodor Dostoyevsky*.

Dostoyevsky, F. (2012). *The grand inquisitor*.

Dowling, B., Lauricella, T., & Schaninger, B. (2021, October 25). *Your return-to-office announcements are missing the mark: Here's how to get them right*. Mckinsey. https://www.mckinsey.com/business-functions/people-and-organizational-performance/our-insights/the-organization-blog/your-return-to-office-announcement-missed-the-mark-heres-how-to-get-it-right

Downs, A. (1997). *Beyond the looking glass: Overcoming the seductive culture of corporate narcissism.* AMACOM.

Dr. A. et al. v. Kathy Hochul, Governor of New York, et al. 595 U. S. _____ (cert. denied), (2021).

Dr. Reality - Dave Champion. (2021, December 3). *They're finally admitting endless jabs needed to get on-going protection.* Youtube. https://www.youtube.com/watch?v=rW-2Rz4wlCw

Drucker, P. F. (1978). *The age of discontinuity: Guidelines to our changing society.* Harper Torchbooks.

Drucker, P. F., & (with Macuaruello, J. A. . (2008). *Management.* HarperCollins.

Duran, E., & Ivey, A. E. (2019). *Healing the soul wound: Trauma-Informed counseling for indigenous communities* (2nd ed.). Teachers College Press.

Durkee, A. (2021, November 18). *Florida Gov. DeSantis signs sweeping legislation restricting vaccine mandates, school mask rules and more.* Forbes. https://www.forbes.com/sites/alisondurkee/2021/11/18/florida-gov-desantis-signs-sweeping-legislation-restricting-vaccine-mandates-school-mask-rules-and-more/?sh=1a11a4ba77cf

Dutton, K. (2012). *The wisdom of psychopaths: What saints, spies, and serial killers can teach us about success.* Macmillan Audio.

Earle, P. C. (Ed.). (2021). *Coronavirus and human rights.* American Institute for Economic Research.

Eberhardt, J. L. (2019). *Biased: Uncovering the hidden prejudice that shapes what we see, think, and do.* Penguin Books.

Eddy, M. (2021, November 20). *Thousands in Austria protest virus lockdown and vaccine mandate.* The New York Times. https://www.nytimes.com/2021/11/20/world/europe/austria-lockdown-vaccine-mandate-covid.html

Editorial Board. (2021, December 9). *Biden's federal vaccine mandate wipeout.* The Wall Street Journal. https://www.wsj.com/articles/bidens-covid-vaccine-mandate-wipeout-courts-11639076342

Edmondson, A. C. (2019). *The fearless organization: Creating psychological safety in the workplace for learning, innovation, and growth* (1st ed.). John Wiley & Sons.

Edsall, T. B. (2021, December 15). *How to tell when your country is past the point of no return.* The New York Times. https://www.nytimes.com/2021/12/15/opinion/republicans-democracy-minority-rule.html

Egan, M. (2022, January 4). *NYC Mayor Eric Adams to big banks: We need you back in the office.* Cable News Network (CNN). https://www.cnn.com/2022/01/04/economy/eric-adams-covid-banks/index.html

Ehrenreich, B. (2005). *Bait and switch: The (futile) pursuit of the American Dream.* Metropolitan Books.

Ekman, P. (1992). *Telling lies: Clues to deceit in the marketplace, politics, and marriage.* W. W. Norton & Company.

Ekman, P. (2009). *Telling lies: Clues to deceit in the marketplace, politics, and marriage (Revised edition).* W. W. Norton & Company.

Elias, J. (2021a, November 23). *Several hundred Google employees sign manifesto against widened Covid vaccine mandate.* CNBC. https://www.cnbc.com/2021/11/23/google-employees-sign-manifesto-against-widened-vaccine-mandate.html

Elias, J. (2021b, December 15). *Google tells employees they'll lose pay and will eventually be fired if they don't follow vaccination rules.* CNBC. https://www.cnbc.com/2021/12/14/google-employees-to-lose-pay-if-dont-comply-with-vaccination-policy.html

Elkington, J., Hartigan, P., & Schwab, K. (2008). *The power of unreasonable people: How social entrepreneurs create markets that change the world.* Harvard Business Review Press.

Ellyatt, H. (2021, December 7). *WHO wades into vaccine mandates dispute, saying they should be an 'absolute last resort.'* CNBC. https://www.cnbc.com/2021/12/07/who-on-vaccine-mandates-they-should-be-a-last-resort.html

Eminem Music. (2010, September 15). *Eminem - The real Slim Shady.* Youtube. https://www.youtube.com/watch?v=eJO5HU_7_1w

Epstein, H. (2019). *Children of the Holocaust: Conversations with sons and daughters of survivors.* Penguin Books.

European Agency for Safety and Health at Work. (2016, October 16). *Occupational safety and health risk assessment methodologies.* https://oshwiki.eu/wiki/Occupational_safety_and_health_risk_asse ssment_methodologies

European Agency for Safety and Health at Work. (2020, December 23). *COVID-19: Back to the workplace - Adapting workplaces and protecting workers.* https://oshwiki.eu/wiki/COVID-19:_Back_to_the_workplace_-_Adapting_workplaces_and_protecting_workers

European Medicines Agency. (2022, January 11). *EMA press briefing 11 January 2022.* Youtube. https://www.youtube.com/watch?v=c_bdtDczwK0&t=51s

Eyal, N., & (with Hoover, R. (2014). *Hooked: How to build habit-forming products* (1st ed.). Portfolio.

Eyewitness News. (2021, December 18). *COVID News: New York sets another single-day positive case record; with nearly 22,000 positive cases.* ABC7NY.Com. https://abc7ny.com/new-york-pop-up-vaccination-sites-covid-spike-omicron-surge/11355479/

Faranda, F. (2020). *The fear paradox: How our obsession with feeling secure imprisons our minds and shapes our lives.* Mango.

Federman, J. (2022, January 16). *Israel study: 4th vaccine shows limited results with omicron.* Associated Press. https://apnews.com/article/coronavirus-pandemic-health-middle-east-israel-5da0bbef16209e9c55e48af40248af11

Feldscher, K. (2021, August 11). *What will it be like when COVID-19 becomes endemic?* Harvard T. C. Chan School of Public Health. https://www.hsph.harvard.edu/news/features/what-will-it-be-like-when-covid-19-becomes-endemic/

Ferguson, N. (2008). *The pity of war: Explaining World War I* (Revised). Basic Books.

Fertik, M., & Thompson, D. C. (2015). *The reputation economy: How to optimize your digital footprint in a world where your reputation is your most valuable asset.* Currency.

Fetters, A. (2020, April 29). *Friends are breaking up over social distancing.* The Atlantic. https://www.theatlantic.com/family/archive/2020/04/friends-are-breaking-up-over-social-distancing/610783/

Fieldstadt, E., Gostanian, A., & Britton, B. (2021, December 6). *900 Better.com employees learn their jobs are being eliminated in a Zoom call.* NBCNews.Com. https://www.nbcnews.com/business/business-news/900-bettercom-employees-learn-jobs-are-eliminated-zoom-call-rcna7738

Fink, S. (2013). *Crisis communications: The definitive guide to managing the message* (1st ed.). McGraw-Hill Education.

Firfiray, S. (2018, November 22). *Microchip implants are threatening workers' rights.* The Conversation. https://theconversation.com/microchip-implants-are-threatening-workers-rights-107221

Fitzpatrick, M. (2006). The Cutter Incident: How America's first polio vaccine led to a growing vaccine crisis. *Journal of the Royal Society of Medicine, 99*(3), 156.

Fitzsimmons, E. G. (2021, December 31). *De Blasio's costly legacy: The biggest city work force ever.* The New York Times. https://www.nytimes.com/2021/12/31/nyregion/de-blasio-budget-unions-nyc.html

Fleischer, R. (1973). *Soylent green.* Metro-Goldwyn-Mayer (MGM).

Fliesler, N. (2016, September 8). *Keeping up with HIV mutations.* Harvard Medical School. https://hms.harvard.edu/news/keeping-hiv-mutations

Forbes Human Resources Council. (2018, June 18). *11 ways to gracefully handle employee termination.* Forbes. https://www.forbes.com/sites/forbeshumanresourcescouncil/2018/06/18/11-ways-to-gracefully-handle-employee-termination/?sh=449b00c93729

Fortier, M. (2021, November 10). *Breakthrough COVID cases up 44% in Massachusetts.* NBCBoston.Com. https://www.nbcboston.com/news/local/breakthrough-covid-cases-in-massachusetts-up-44/2561754/

Foster, G., Frijters, P., & Baker, M. (2021). *The Great Covid Panic: What happened, why, and what to do next.* Brownstone Institute.

Frank, A. J., & Wilson, E. A. (2020). *A Silvan Tomkins handbook: Foundations for affect theory.* University of Minnesota Press.

Franke, N. (2021). *Built to belong: Discovering the power of community over competition*. Worthy Books.

Frankfurt, H. G. (2005). *On bullshit*. Recorded Books.

Fraser, N. (2017). Behind Marx's hidden abode: For an expanded conception of capitalism. In *Critical theory in critical times* (pp. 141–159). Columbia University Press. https://doi.org/10.7312/columbia/9780231181518.003.0007

Freeman, R. E. (2010). *Strategic management: A stakeholder approach*. Cambridge University Press.

Fritzon, K., Brooks, N., & Croom, S. (2019). *Corporate psychopathy: Investigating destructive personalities in the workplace* (1st ed.). Palgrave Macmillan.

Fromm, E. (2010). *On disobedience: 'Why freedom means saying "no" to power*. HarperCollins.

Fryhofer, S. (2021, October 26). *Sandra Fryhofer, MD, discusses new "mix & match strategy" for boosters*. American Medical Association. https://www.ama-assn.org/delivering-care/public-health/sandra-fryhofer-md-discusses-new-mix-match-strategy-boosters

Fullbrook, E., & Morgan, J. (Eds.). (2021). *Post-Neoliberal economics*. World Economics Association Books.

Fullenkamp, C. (2015). *The economics of uncertainty*. Great Courses.

Fuller, E. (2011). *You can't lead with your feet on the desk: Building relationships, breaking down barriers, and delivering profits* (1st ed.). John Wiley & Sons.

Fuller, P., Murphy, M., & (with Chow, A. (2020). *The leader's guide to unconscious bias: How to reframe bias, cultivate connection, and create high-performing teams*. Simon & Schuster.

Fuller, R. W. (n.d.). *Rankism*. Breaking Ranks. https://www.breakingranks.net/rankism/

Fuller, R. W. (2004). *Somebodies and nobodies: Overcoming the abuse of rank*. New Society Publishers.

Fuller, R. W. (2013, August 11). *Curing the poison of "rankism."* Psychology Today. https://www.psychologytoday.com/us/blog/somebodies-and-nobodies/201308/curing-the-poison-rankism

Galbraith, J. K., & Galbraith, J. K. (2009). *The great crash 1929* (1st ed.).

Mariner Books.

Gamble, J. E., Thompson, A. A., & Peteraf, M. A. (2018). *Essentials of strategic management: The quest for competitive advantage* (6th ed.). McGraw-Hill Higher Education.

Gan, N. (2021, December 30). *Alleged Chinese smugglers publicly shamed for breaching Covid rules.* Cable News Network (CNN). https://www.cnn.com/2021/12/30/china/china-public-shaming-parade-intl-hnk/index.html

Gardner, H. (2006). *Changing minds: The art and science of changing our own and other people's minds* (First Trade Paper). Harvard Business Review Press.

Garrick, J. (2012, June 1). *Demanding fairness on the job – New uses for an old law.* Scholars Strategy Network. https://scholars.org/contribution/demanding-fairness-job-new-uses-old-law

Gatopoulos, D. (2022, January 17). *In Greece, unvaccinated people 60 and up face monthly fines.* Associated Press. https://apnews.com/article/coronavirus-pandemic-health-europe-greece-public-health-833c28b931b227fb91f2a5430bb32a2a

Gavett, G. (2021, September 28). *The problem with "greedy work."* Harvard Business Review. https://hbr.org/2021/09/the-problem-with-greedy-work

Geiling, N. (2013, December). The confusing and at-times counterproductive 1980s response to the AIDS epidemic. *Smithsonian Magazine.* https://www.smithsonianmag.com/history/the-confusing-and-at-times-counterproductive-1980s-response-to-the-aids-epidemic-180948611/

Gelles, D., & Goldberg, E. (2021, December 31). *Business leaders struggle with endless upheaval.* The New York Times. https://www.nytimes.com/2021/12/31/business/ceos-pandemic-leadership.html

Gellman, B. (2021, December 6). *Trump's next coup has already begun.* The Atlantic. https://www.theatlantic.com/magazine/archive/2022/01/january-6-insurrection-trump-coup-2024-election/620843/

Ghaemi, S. N. (2011). *A first-rate madness: Uncovering the links between leadership and mental illness.* Penguin Books.

Ghebreyesus, T. A. (2020, March 11). *WHO Director-General's opening remarks at the media briefing on COVID-19 - 11 March 2020*. World Health Organization (WHO). https://www.who.int/director-general/speeches/detail/who-director-general-s-opening-remarks-at-the-media-briefing-on-covid-19---11-march-2020

Ghebreyesus, T. A. (2021, December 22). *WHO Director-General's opening remarks at the media briefing on COVID-19 - 22 December 2021*. World Health Organization (WHO). https://www.who.int/director-general/speeches/detail/who-director-general-s-opening-remarks-at-the-media-briefing-on-covid-19---22-december-2021

Gilbert, S., & Green, C. (2021). *Vaxxers: The inside story of the Oxford AstraZeneca Vaccine and the race against the virus*. Hodder & Stoughton.

Giles, D. (2010). *Psychology of the media* (N. Holt & R. Lewis (Eds.); 1st ed.). Bloomsbury Academic.

Gingrich, N. (2020). *Trump and the American future: Solving the great problems of our time*. Center Street.

Gipson-Fine, A. (2022, January 12). *Beyond "I'm sorry": Employers need to manage grief, trauma in the workplace*. The Hill. https://thehill.com/opinion/healthcare/589241-beyond-im-sorry-employers-need-to-manage-grief-trauma-in-the-workplace

Goffman, E. (2009). *Stigma: Notes on the management of spoiled identity* (Reissue). Touchstone.

Goldberg, E. (2022, January 25). *OSHA withdraws its workplace vaccine rule*. The New York Times. https://www.nytimes.com/2022/01/25/business/osha-vaccine-mandate.html?searchResultPosition=1

Goldberg, E., Hirsch, L., & McCabe, D. (2022, January 12). *Why some workers are getting all the Covid tests they need*. The New York Times. https://www.nytimes.com/2022/01/12/business/covid-testing-google-blackrock-morgan-stanley.html

Goldberg, M. (2021, December 4). *Goldberg: What 'my body, my choice' means to the right*. Austin American-Statesman. https://www.statesman.com/story/opinion/2021/12/04/goldberg-what-my-body-my-choice-means-right/8828589002/

Goldberg, Y., Mandel, M., Bar-On, Y. M., Bodenheimer, O., Freedman, L., Haas, E. J., Milo, R., Alroy-Preis, S., Ash, N., & Huppert, A. (2021).

Waning immunity after the BNT162b2 vaccine in Israel. *New England Journal of Medicine, 385*(24), e85. https://doi.org/10.1056/NEJMoa2114228

Gostick, A., & Elton, C. (2021). *Anxiety at work: 8 strategies to help teams build resilience, handle uncertainty, and get stuff done.* Harper Business.

Gottlieb, S. (2021). *Uncontrolled spread: Why COVID-19 crushed us and how we can defeat the next pandemic.* Harper.

Graham, R. (2021, December 10). *A majority of Americans are critical of religious exemptions to Covid vaccines, a survey finds.* The New York Times. https://www.nytimes.com/2021/12/10/us/us-religious-covid-vaccines-mandate.html

Grant, A. M. (2021a). *Think again: The power of knowing what you don't know.* Viking.

Grant, A. M. (2021b, September). *Adam Grant posted on LinkedIn.* LinkedIn. https://www.linkedin.com/posts/adammgrant_activity-6845699655926390784-wyyO

Gratton, L. (2021, December 21). *Why it's so hard to keep and recruit employees right now.* MIT Salon Management Review. https://sloanreview.mit.edu/article/why-its-so-hard-to-keep-and-recruit-employees-right-now/

Greene, R., & Elffers, J. (2003). *The art of seduction.* Penguin Books.

Greifeneder, R., Jaffe, M., Newman, E., & Schwarz, N. (Eds.). (2020). *The psychology of fake news: Accepting, sharing, and correcting misinformation* (1st ed.). Routledge.

Grimm, A. (2015, September 5). *A decade after Danziger Bridge shooting, killings still cast a shadow.* Nola.Com. https://www.nola.com/news/crime_police/article_00bb8d39-aa35-5959-b613-873905a4e734.html

Griswold v. Connecticut, 381 U.S. 479, (1965).

Gross, J. T. (2007). *Fear: Anti-Semitism in Poland after Auschwitz* (1st ed.). Random House.

Guadalupe, M., Kinias, Z., & Schloderer, F. (2021). *Aligning individual and organisational values.* Insead Knowledge. https://knowledge.insead.edu/leadership-organisations/aligning-individual-and-organisational-values-17561

Gupta, S. (2021). *Childhood, interrupted: Raising kids during a pandemic.* Audible Originals.

Hadnagy, C. (2018). *Social engineering: The science of human hacking* (2nd ed.). John Wiley & Sons.

Hadnagy, C., & Schulman, S. (2021). *Human hacking: Win friends, influence people, and leave them better off for having met you.* Harper Business.

Haidt, J. (2012). *The righteous mind: Why good people are divided by politics and religion* (1st ed.). Vintage.

Hales, D., Hales, R. E., & Frances, A. (1995). *Caring for the mind: The comprehensive guide to mental health.* Bantam Books.

Hallowell, N. (2014). *Driven to distraction at work: How to focus and be more productive* (1st ed.). Harvard Business Review Press.

Halperin, E. (2015). *Emotions in conflict: Inhibitors and facilitators of peace making* (1st ed.). Routledge.

Hanna, J., & Holcombe, M. (2021, July 30). *American workers are facing increasing pressure to get vaccinated against Covid-19.* Cable News Network (CNN). https://www.cnn.com/2021/07/29/health/us-coronavirus-thursday/index.html

Hannah, D. R., Zatzick, C. D., & Kietzmann, J. (2021). Turbulent times demand dynamic rules. *MIT Sloan Management Review, 62*(4), 60–65. https://sloanreview.mit.edu/article/turbulent-times-demand-dynamic-rules/?og=Summer+2021+Issue+Tiled

Hardy, B. P. (2018). *Willpower doesn't work: Discover the hidden keys to success.* Hachette Books.

Harfoush, R. (2019). *Hustle and float: Reclaim your creativity and thrive in a world obsessed with work.* Diversion Books.

Harfoush, R. (2021, November 12). *Don't let returning to the office burn out your team.* Harvard Business Review. https://hbr.org/2021/11/dont-let-returning-to-the-office-burn-out-your-team

Harlan, C. (2021, December 18). *Highly vaccinated countries thought they were over the worst. Denmark says the pandemic's toughest month is just beginning.* The Washington Post. https://www.washingtonpost.com/world/2021/12/18/omicron-variant-denmark/

Harris, C. (2021, November 30). *Most employers will require workers to get COVID-19 shots, survey shows.* USA Today. https://www.usatoday.com/story/money/2021/11/30/vaccination-mandates-most-employers-require-covid-shots/8798203002/

Harsh, S. (2020). *The pandemic war: 12 Guaranteed ways to fail!*

Harvard Graduate School of Education. (2017, October 4). *Askwith forum: Cornel West – Spiritual blackout, imperial meltdown, prophetic fightback [Video].* Youtube. https://www.youtube.com/watch?v=zuxqhsrCGeg&t=1235s

Healy, J., Weiland, N., & Fausset, R. (2021, December 25). *As Omicron spreads and cases soar, the unvaccinated remain defiant.* The New York Times. https://www.nytimes.com/2021/12/25/us/omicron-unvaccinated.html

Heckenlively, K. (2021). *Case against vaccine mandates.* Hot Books.

Hedges, C. (2010). *Death of the liberal class* (1st ed.). Bold Type Books.

Heery, E., & Noon, M. (2017). *A dictionary of human resource management* (3rd ed.). Oxford University Press.

Heffernan, M. (2011). *Willful blindness: Why we ignore the obvious at our peril.* Bloomsbury USA.

Heller, J. (2021, December 30). *Israel approves fourth COVID-19 vaccine shot for most vulnerable.* Reuters. https://www.reuters.com/world/middle-east/top-israeli-health-official-approves-second-covid-19-vaccine-booster-2021-12-30/

Herman, E. S., & Chomsky, N. (2011). *Manufacturing consent: The political economy of the mass media.* Pantheon.

Heskett, J. L. (2021, November 1). *How long does it take to improve an organization's culture?* Harvard Business School Working Knowledge. https://hbswk.hbs.edu/item/how-long-does-it-take-to-improve-an-organizations-culture

Heskett, J. L. (2022). *Win from within: Build organizational culture for competitive advantage.* Columbia Business School Publishing.

Heying, H., & Weinstein, B. (2021). *A hunter-gatherer's guide to the 21st century: Evolution and the challenges of modern life.* Portfolio.

Heyward, G. (2021, November 29). *A judge temporarily blocks a vaccine mandate for health workers in 10 states.* The New York Times. https://www.nytimes.com/2021/11/29/us/judge-blocks-vaccine-mandate.html

Hibbert, N. (2019). *Just f*cking do it: Stop playing small. Transform your life.* John Murray.

Hicks, D. (2018). *Leading with dignity: How to create a culture that brings out the best in people.* Yale University Press.

Hicks, S. R. C. (2010). *Nietzsche and the Nazis* (1st ed.). Ockham's Razor.

Hill. (2021, November 16). *Kim Iversen: Unvaccinated in lockdown in Austria, will the US be next?* YouTube. https://www.youtube.com/watch?v=WcB8N_gdc-o&t=336s

Hodge, J. (2022, January 7). *Supreme Court considers derailing federal vaccine mandates – appears inclined to keep for health workers, but not wider workforce.* The Conversation. https://theconversation.com/supreme-court-considers-derailing-federal-vaccine-mandates-appears-inclined-to-keep-for-health-workers-but-not-wider-workforce-174461

Holt-Lunstad, J., Smith, T. B., & Layton, J. B. (2010). Social relationships and mortality risk: A meta-analytic review. *PLoS Medicine, 7*(7), e1000316. https://doi.org/10.1371/journal.pmed.1000316

Horowitz, L. G., & Martin, W. J. (2018). *Emerging viruses: AIDS and Ebola: Nature, accident, or intentional?* Tetrahedron Media.

Hougaard, R., & Carter, J. (2021, November 23). *Becoming a more humane leader.* Harvard Business Review. https://hbr.org/2021/11/becoming-a-more-humane-leader?ab=hero-main-text

Hougaard, R., Carter, J., & Afton, M. (2021, December 23). *Connect with empathy, but lead with compassion.* Harvard Business Review. https://hbr.org/2021/12/connect-with-empathy-but-lead-with-compassion

Hougaard, R., Carter, J., & Hobson, N. (2020, December 4). *Compassionate leadership is necessary — but not sufficient.* Harvard Business Review. https://hbr.org/2020/12/compassionate-leadership-is-necessary-but-not-sufficient

Howell, J. L., & Sweeny, K. (2016). Is waiting bad for subjective health? *Journal of Behavioral Medicine, 39*(4), 652–664.

https://doi.org/10.1007/s10865-016-9729-7

Hsu, A. (2021, November 4). *Biden's vaccine rules for 100 million workers are here. These are the details.* National Public Radio (NPR). https://www.npr.org/2021/11/04/1048939858/osha-biden-vaccine-mandate-employers-100-workers

Hübl, T., Avritt, J. J., & Ury, W. (2020). *Healing collective trauma: A process for integrating our intergenerational and cultural wounds.* Sounds True.

Hubler, E. (1999, January 3). *The new faces of retirement.* The New York Times. https://www.nytimes.com/1999/01/03/business/the-new-faces-of-retirement.html?searchResultPosition=16

Hubler, S., & Harmon, A. (2021, December 18). *As Covid surges, experts say U.S. booster effort is far behind.* The New York Times. https://www.nytimes.com/2021/12/18/us/omicron-booster-shots-americans.html

Hudson, F. M., & McLean, P. D. (2006). *Life launch: A passionate guide to the rest of your life* (4th ed.). Hudson Institute Press.

Hudson, P. (2021, November 12). *Sanofi CEO Paul Hudson on company culture in a distributed office.* Harvard Business Review. https://hbr.org/2021/11/sanofi-ceo-paul-hudson-on-company-culture-in-a-distributed-office

Hughes, R. L., Ginnette, R. C., & Curphy, G. J. (2012). *Leadership: Enhancing the lessons of experience* (6th ed.). McGraw-Hill/Irwin.

Hupka, S. (2021, May 25). *No, it is not illegal for businesses to require proof of vaccination.* Capradio. https://www.capradio.org/articles/2021/05/25/no-it-is-not-illegal-for-businesses-to-require-proof-of-vaccination/

Hutzler, A. (2021, October 7). *These media personalities have stepped away from their jobs over vaccine mandate.* Newsweek. https://www.newsweek.com/these-media-personalities-have-stepped-away-their-jobs-over-vaccine-mandate-1636565

Ibarra, H. (2019). Take a wrecking ball to your company's iconic practices. *MIT Sloan Management Review, 61*(2), 13–16. https://sloanreview.mit.edu/article/take-a-wrecking-ball-to-your-companys-iconic-practices/?og=Frontiers+Series

Ingram, D. (2022, January 14). *National digital vaccine card aims to ease proof   of   vaccination   requirements.*   Today. https://www.today.com/news/national-digital-vaccine-card-aims-ease-proof-vaccination-requirements-rcna12218

International Institute for Democracy and Electoral Assistance. (2021). *The global state of democracy 2021: Building resilience in a pandemic era.* https://doi.org/10.31752/idea.2021.91

International Institute of Democracy and Electoral Assistance. (2021, November 22). *Democracy faces perfect storm as the world becomes more authoritarian.* Idea.Int. https://www.idea.int/news-media/news/democracy-faces-perfect-storm-world-becomes-more-authoritarian

International Space Station National Laboratory (ISS). (n.d.). *History and timeline of the ISS.* https://www.issnationallab.org/about/iss-timeline/

Ivancevich, J. M. (2010). *Human resource management* (11th ed.). McGraw-Hill/Irwin.

Jackson, M., & McKibben, B. (2008). *Distracted: The erosion of attention and the coming dark age.* Prometheus.

Jacobson v. Massachusetts, 197 U.S. 11, (1905).

Jaffe, S. (2021). *Work won't love you back: How devotion to our jobs keeps us exploited, exhausted, and alone.* Bold Type Books.

Jähner, H. (2022). *Aftermath: Life in the fallout of the Third Reich, 1945-1955.* Knopf.

Jeong, A., & Suliman, A. (2021, December 9). *Omicron may require fourth vaccine dose sooner than expected, Pfizer says.* The Washington Post. https://www.washingtonpost.com/nation/2021/12/09/covid-omicron-variant-live-updates/

Jex, S. M., & Britt, T. W. (2014). *Organizational psychology: A scientist-practitioner approach* (3rd ed.). John Wiley & Sons.

John Does 1–3, et al. v. Janet T. Mills, Governor of Maine, et al. 595 U. S. _____, (2021).

Johnson, E. J. (2021). *The elements of choice: Why the way we decide matters.* Riverhead Books.

Jones, J. (2021, March 19). *5 facts about the state of the gender pay gap.*

U.S. Department of Labor Blog. https://blog.dol.gov/2021/03/19/5-facts-about-the-state-of-the-gender-pay-gap

Jung, C. G. (1964). After the catastrophe. In H. Read, M. Fordham, & G. Adler (Eds.), *The collected works: Civilization in transition: Vol. 10* (2nd ed., pp. 194–217). Pantheon Books.

Jung, C. G. (2014). *Collected works of C.G. Jung, Volume 11: Psychology and religion: West and East* (H. Read, M. Fordham, & G. Adler (Eds.); 2nd ed.). Princeton University Press.

Kabat-Zinn, J. (2013). *Full catastrophe living: Using the wisdom of your body and mind to face stress, pain, and illness* (Revised). Bantam Books.

Kadushin, C. (2012). *Understanding social networks: Theories, concepts, and findings* (Illustrate). Oxford University Press.

Kallingal, M., & Boyette, C. (2021, December 3). *Nurse charged with making fake Covid-19 vaccine cards.* Cable News Network (CNN). https://www.cnn.com/2021/12/03/us/nurse-charged-fake-vaccine-cards/index.html

Karp, M. (2018, February 19). *WTF happened to Government Cheese?* Vice. https://www.vice.com/en/article/wn7mgq/wtf-happened-to-government-cheese

Karpman, S. B. (1968). Fairy tales and script drama analysis. *Transactional Analysis Bulletin, 7*(26), 39–43.

Karpman, S. B. (2007, August 11). *The new drama triangles.* Karpman Drama Triangle. https://karpmandramatriangle.com/pdf/thenewdramatriangles.pdf

Kaufman, J. (2012). *The personal MBA: Master the art of business.* Portfolio/Penguin.

Keith, T. (2021, October 4). *119 out of 26,500 employees terminated because of UCHealth COVID-19 vaccine requirement in Colorado.* KKTV 11 News. https://www.kktv.com/2021/10/04/119-out-26500-employees-terminated-because-uchealth-covid-19-vaccine-requirement-colorado/

Kennedy, R. F. J. (2021). *The real Anthony Fauci: Bill Gates, big pharma, and the global war on democracy and public health.* Skyhorse.

Keyes, R. (2004). *The post-truth era: Dishonesty and deception in contemporary life*. St. Martin's Press.

Kierkegaard, S. (2019). *The Kierkegaard collection*. Blackmore Dennett.

Kimball, S. (2021a, December 3). *WHO says Covid omicron variant detected in 38 countries, early data suggests it's more contagious than delta*. CNBC. https://www.cnbc.com/2021/12/03/who-says-omicron-covid-variant-has-spread-to-38-countries.html

Kimball, S. (2021b, December 7). *Omicron significantly reduces Covid antibody protection in small study of Pfizer vaccine recipients*. CNBC. https://www.cnbc.com/2021/12/07/omicron-significantly-reduces-covid-antibody-protection-in-small-study-of-pfizer-vaccine-recipients.html

Kimball, S. (2021c, December 7). *U.S. court temporarily halts Biden's vaccine mandate for federal contractors nationwide*. CNBC. https://www.cnbc.com/2021/12/07/us-court-temporarily-halts-bidens-vaccine-mandate-for-federal-contractors.html

Kimball, S. (2021d, December 8). *Pfizer CEO says fourth Covid vaccine doses may be needed sooner than expected due to omicron*. CNBC. https://www.cnbc.com/2021/12/08/omicron-pfizer-ceo-says-we-may-need-fourth-covid-vaccine-doses-sooner-than-expected.html

King, W. C., Rubinstein, M., Reinhart, A., & Mejia, R. J. (2021, October 25). *Time trends, factors associated with, and reasons for COVID-19 vaccine hesitancy in US adults: January-May 2021*. MeDrxiv. https://doi.org/10.1101/2021.07.20.21260795

Klotz, A. (2021, September 2). *Anthony Klotz on defining the Great Resignation*. The Verse Media. https://www.theversemedia.com/articles/anthony-klotz-defining-the-great-resignation

Kovaleski, S. F. (2021, January 5). *Second doses have begun for the earliest U.S. vaccine recipients*. The New York Times. https://www.nytimes.com/2021/01/05/us/second-doses-have-begun-for-the-earliest-us-vaccine-recipients.html?searchResultPosition=45

Kriegel, R. J., & Brandt, D. (1997). *Sacred Cows make the best burgers: Developing change-driving people and organizations* (1st ed.). Warner Business Books.

Krugman, P. (2009). *The return of depression economics and the crisis of 2008*. W. W. Norton & Company.

Kubler-Ross, E., & Kessler, D. (2005). *On grief and grieving: Finding the meaning of grief through the Five Stages of Loss* (1st ed.). Scribner.

Kurtzman, J., Rifkin, G., & Griffith, V. (2004). *MBA in a book: Mastering business with attitude*. Three Rivers Press.

Lamneck, K. (2020, June 24). *Technology promises a safer return to work, but don't forget the (virtual) human touch*. Forbes. https://www.forbes.com/sites/forbestechcouncil/2020/06/24/techn ology-promises-a-safer-return-to-work-but-dont-forget-the-virtual-human-touch/?sh=2c3f2e9d6804

Landler, M. (2021, December 10). *Vaccine mandates rekindle fierce debate over civil liberties*. The New York Times. https://www.nytimes.com/2021/12/10/world/europe/vaccine-mandates-civil-liberties.html

Lauren, P. G. (2013). *The rights of man: Great thinkers and great movements*. Great Courses.

Lenderman, E. A., & Langham, R. Y. (2019). *Human capital management: A brief review of HR, organizational psychology, and economic systems*.

Lenin, V. I. (2021). *Imperialism the highest stage of capitalism*. Sanage Publishing House.

Levin-Scherz, J., & Toro, P. (2021, December 3). *The Omicron variant: How companies should respond*. Harvard Business Review. https://hbr.org/2021/12/the-omicron-variant-how-companies-should-respond?ab=hero-main-text

Levitsky, S., & Ziblatt, D. (2018). *How democracies die* (Reprint). Crown.

Levy, J., Klein, J. I., Rice, C., & Haass, R. N. (2012). U.S. education reform and national security. In *Council on Foreign Relations Press*. https://cdn.cfr.org/sites/default/files/report_pdf/TFR68_Education _National_Security.pdf

Levy, R. H. (2020). *Mending America's political divide: What science tells us about solving the political hatred between the left and the right*. USA Peoplehood Press.

Liebermann, O. (2021, December 13). *Air Force discharges 27 troops for refusing Covid-19 vaccine*. Cable News Network (CNN). https://www.cnn.com/2021/12/13/politics/air-force-troops-discharged-covid-19-vaccine/index.html

Lifton, R. J. (2012). *Thought reform and the psychology of totalism: A study of "brainwashing" in China.* University of North Carolina Press.

Lind, E. A., & Tyler, T. R. (2013). *The social psychology of procedural justice* (1988th ed.). Springer.

Lindstrom, M., & Spurlock, M. (2011). *Brandwashed: Tricks companies use to manipulate our minds and persuade us to buy.* Currency.

Liptak, A. (2022a, January 7). *Conservative majority on Supreme Court appears skeptical of Biden's virus plan.* The New York Times. https://www.nytimes.com/2022/01/07/us/politics/biden-vaccine-mandate-supreme-court.html

Liptak, A. (2022b, January 13). *Supreme court blocks Biden's virus mandate for large employers.* The New York Times. https://www.nytimes.com/2022/01/13/us/politics/supreme-court-biden-vaccine-mandate.html

Liu, L., Iketani, S., Guo, Y., Chan, J. F.-W., Wang, M., Liu, L., Luo, Y., Chu, H., Huang, Y., Nair, M. S., Yu, J., Chik, K. K.-H., Yuen, T. T.-T., Yoon, C., To, K. K.-W., Chen, H., Yin, M. T., Sobieszczyk, M. E., Huang, Y., ... Ho, D. D. (2021). Striking antibody evasion manifested by the Omicron variant of SARS-CoV-2. *BioRxiv,* 2021.12.14.472719. https://doi.org/10.1101/2021.12.14.472719

Lopez, G. (2016, December 1). *The Reagan administration's unbelievable response to the HIV/AIDS epidemic.* Vox. https://www.vox.com/2015/12/1/9828348/ronald-reagan-hiv-aids

Lord, E. (2014). *The great plague: A people's history.* Yale University Press.

Lowenthal, B. (1987, October 25). *The jumpers of '29.* The Washington Post. https://www.washingtonpost.com/archive/opinions/1987/10/25/the-jumpers-of-29/17defff9-f725-43b7-831b-7924ac0a1363/

Lubell, J. (2021, November 1). *COVID-19 vaccine boosters mix and match: What the evidence shows.* American Medical Association. https://www.ama-assn.org/delivering-care/public-health/covid-19-vaccine-boosters-mix-and-match-what-evidence-shows

Lufkin, B. (2021, June 7). *Why presenteeism wins out over productivity.* British Broadcasting Corporation (BBC). https://www.bbc.com/worklife/article/20210604-why-presenteeism-always-wins-out-over-productivity

Lumet, S. (1976). *Network.* Metro-Goldwyn-Mayer (MGM).

Lustig, R. H. (2017). *The hacking of the American mind: The science behind the corporate takeover of our bodies and brains.* Avery.

MacArthur, H. V. (2019, April 16). *Treating employees like customers: Why it's your best performance strategy.* Forbes. https://www.forbes.com/sites/hvmacarthur/2019/04/16/treating-employees-like-customers-why-its-your-best-performance-strategy/?sh=36e9e43616ea

Maitlis, S. (2020). Posttraumatic growth at work. *Annual Review of Organizational Psychology and Organizational Behavior, 7*(1), 395–419. https://doi.org/10.1146/annurev-orgpsych-012119-044932

Malone, K., & Duffin, K. (2021, May 21). *Big government cheese (classic).* National Public Radio (NPR). https://www.npr.org/2021/05/21/999144678/big-government-cheese-classic

Mandavilli, A. (2021, November 19). *C.D.C. endorses Covid vaccine booster shots for all adults.* The New York Times. https://www.nytimes.com/2021/11/19/health/covid-boosters-cdc.html

Mandavilli, A. (2022a, January 6). *Will 'forever boosting' beat the coronavirus?* The New York Times. https://www.nytimes.com/2022/01/06/health/covid-vaccines-boosters.html

Mandavilli, A. (2022b, January 27). *An Israeli study finds a slightly higher-than-expected rate of heart problems in vaccinated boys.* The New York Times. https://www.nytimes.com/2022/01/26/health/myocarditis-israel-vaccine-study-boys.html

Mandavilli, A. (2022c, January 27). *Yes, Omicron is loosening its hold. But the pandemic has not ended.* The New York Times. https://www.nytimes.com/2022/01/27/health/omicron-covid-pandemic.html

Manning, M. G. (2014). *When books went to war: The stories that helped us win World War II.* Mariner Books.

Mariner, W. K., Annas, G. J., & Glantz, L. H. (2005). Jacobson v Massachusetts: It's not your great-great-grandfather's public health law. *American Journal of Public Health, 95*(4), 581–590. https://doi.org/10.2105/AJPH.2004.055160

Markson, S. (2021). *What really happened in Wuhan: A virus like no other, countless infections, millions of deaths.* HarperCollins.

Maxouris, C., & Elassar, A. (2022, January 1). *The Covid-19 case surge is altering daily life across the US. Things will likely get worse, experts warn.* Cable News Network (CNN). https://www.cnn.com/2022/01/01/health/us-coronavirus-saturday/index.html

Maxouris, C., & Yan, H. (2022, January 2). *Why this Covid-19 surge is "unprecedented in this pandemic."* Cable News Network (CNN). https://www.cnn.com/2022/01/02/health/us-coronavirus-sunday/index.html

Maxwell, J. C. (2007). *The 21 irrefutable laws of leadership: Follow them and people will follow you.* Thomas Nelson.

May, R. (2009). *Man's search for himself* (Reprint). W. W. Norton & Company.

Mazzei, P. (2021, December 22). *Omicron is just beginning and Americans are already tired.* The New York Times. https://www.nytimes.com/2021/12/22/us/omicron-virus-worry-dread.html

Mazzucato, M. (2018). *The value of everything: Making and taking in the global economy.* Public Affairs.

McCarthy, J. (2021, October 30). *Singapore abandons the "zero COVID" strategy.* National Public Radio (NPR). https://www.npr.org/2021/10/30/1050850666/singapore-abandons-the-zero-covid-strategy

McDonald, M. (2021). *United States of fear: How America fell victim to a mass delusional psychosis.* Bombardier Books.

McGreevy, N. (2021, March 5). *An unexploded WWII bomb was (safely) detonated in England.* Smithsonian Magazine. https://www.smithsonianmag.com/smart-news/unexploded-bomb-wwii-was-safely-detonated-england-180977146/

McGregor, J. (2017, October 4). *This former surgeon general says there's a 'loneliness epidemic' and work is partly to blame.* The Washington Post. https://www.washingtonpost.com/news/on-leadership/wp/2017/10/04/this-former-surgeon-general-says-theres-a-loneliness-epidemic-and-work-is-partly-to-blame/

McMeekin, S. (2014). *July 1914: Countdown to war* (1st ed.). Basic Books.

Meerloo, J. A. M. (2015). *The rape of the mind: The psychology of thought control, menticide, and brainwashing.* Hauraki Publishing.

Merchant, K. A. (1982, July 15). *The control function of management.* MIT Sloan Management Review. https://sloanreview.mit.edu/article/the-control-function-of-management/

Meredith, S. (2021, February 12). *Doctors warn that Covid will become endemic and people need to learn to live with it.* CNBC. https://www.cnbc.com/2021/02/12/doctors-warn-covid-will-become-endemic-and-people-need-to-learn-to-live-with-it.html

Merton, T. (2002). *No man is an island.* Mariner Books.

Meserve, J. (2003, February 11). *Duct tape sales rise amid terror fears.* Cable News Network (CNN). https://edition.cnn.com/2003/US/02/11/emergency.supplies/

Mevorach, D., Anis, E., Cedar, N., Hasin, T., Bromberg, M., Goldberg, L., Parnasa, E., Dichtiar, R., Hershkovitz, Y., Ash, N., Green, M. S., Keinan-Boker, L., & Alroy-Preis, S. (2022). Myocarditis after BNT162b2 vaccination in Israeli adolescents. *New England Journal of Medicine.* https://doi.org/10.1056/NEJMc2116999

Meyer, E. (2014). *The culture map: Breaking through the invisible boundaries of global business.* Public Affairs.

Meyersohn, N. (2022, January 21). *Americans are showing up sick to work even as Omicron spreads.* Cable News Network (CNN). https://www.cnn.com/2022/01/20/economy/paid-sick-leave-covid-retail-restaurant-workers/index.html

Mikovits, J., Heckenlively, K., & Kennedy, R. F. J. (2020). *Plague of corruption: Restoring faith in the promise of science.* Skyhorse.

Milkman, K., & Duckworth, A. (2021). *How to change: The science of getting from where you are to where you want to be.* Portfolio.

Miller, A. M., & Tomlinson, L. Y. (2021, December 30). *More than 200 Marines have been discharged from military due to vaccine refusal.* Fox News Network. https://www.foxnews.com/politics/more-than-200-marines-have-been-discharged-from-military-vaccine-refusal

Miller, K. (2021, October 27). *COVID-19 will likely become an endemic disease—but when will that happen?* Health.

https://www.health.com/condition/infectious-diseases/coronavirus/endemic-covid

Miller, K. L. (2021, September 30). *During the 'Great Resignation,' workers refuse to accept the unacceptable.* The Washington Post. https://www.washingtonpost.com/business/2021/09/30/during-great-resignation-workers-refuse-accept-unacceptable/

MIT SMR Strategy Forum. (2021, October 27). *Will relaxed rules about hybrid work improve productivity and performance?* MIT Salon Management Review. https://sloanreview.mit.edu/strategy-forum/will-relaxed-rules-about-hybrid-work-improve-productivity-and-performance/?utm_source=newsletter&utm_medium=email&utm_content=Read the new forum now »&utm_campaign=Enews Gen 11/2/2021

Mitchell, A. (2021, October 22). *The future of work is hybrid – here's an expert's recommendations.* The Conversation. https://theconversation.com/the-future-of-work-is-hybrid-heres-an-experts-recommendations-167432

Moreland, A., Herlihy, C., Tynan, M. A., Sunshine, G., McCord, R. F., Hilton, C., Poovey, J., Werner, A. K., Jones, C. D., Fulmer, E. B., Gundlapalli, A. V., Strosnider, H., Potvien, A., García, M. C., Honeycutt, S., Baldwin, G., Clodfelter, C., Howard-Williams, M., Jeong, G., ... Popoola, A. (2020). Timing of state and territorial COVID-19 stay-at-home orders and changes in population movement — United States, March 1–May 31, 2020. *MMWR. Morbidity and Mortality Weekly Report, 69*(35), 1198–1203. https://doi.org/10.15585/mmwr.mm6935a2

Morin, A. (2021, November 30). *What is a psychopath?* VeryWell Mind. https://www.verywellmind.com/what-is-a-psychopath-5025217

Morris, A. (2022, January 3). *When three shots are not enough.* Cable News Network (CNN). https://www.nytimes.com/2022/01/03/us/additional-doses-covid-vaccine.html

Morse, B. (2021, November 7). *What's next for Aaron Rodgers and the Green Bay Packers?* Cable News Network (CNN). https://www.cnn.com/2021/11/07/sport/aaron-rodgers-covid-19-follow-up-spt-intl/index.html

Mounk, Y. (2021, December 22). *Omicron is the beginning of the end.* The Atlantic. https://www.theatlantic.com/ideas/archive/2021/12/omicron-end-of-pandemic/621089/

Mutter, J. (2016, April 18). *Opportunity from crisis*. Foreign Affairs. https://www.foreignaffairs.com/articles/2016-04-18/opportunity-crisis

Myers, D. G. (2005). *Social psychology* (8th ed.). McGraw-Hill.

Nagele-Piazza, L. (2021, December 9). *What to expect from OSHA on COVID-19 vaccine and testing rules*. Society for Human Resource Management (SHRM). https://www.shrm.org/resourcesandtools/legal-and-compliance/employment-law/pages/what-to-expect-from-osha-on-covid-19-vaccine-and-testing-rules.aspx

Nathan-Kazis, J. (2022, January 12). *A booster vaccine red flag: Getting too many could backfire*. Barron's. https://www.barrons.com/articles/repeat-covid-vaccine-booster-shots-51642026102?tesla=y

National Aeronautics and Space Administration (NASA). (2019, June 20). *July 20, 1969: One giant leap For mankind*. https://www.nasa.gov/mission_pages/apollo/apollo11.html

National Federation of Independent Business, et al. v. Department of Labor - Occupational Safety and Health Administration, et al. 595 U. S. ____, (2022).

National WWII Museum. (1970, May 7). *The end of World War II 1945*. https://www.nationalww2museum.org/war/topics/end-world-war-ii-1945

Neeley, T. (2022, January 14). *Tsedal Neeley on why we need to think of the office as a tool, with very specific uses*. Harvard Business Review. https://hbr.org/2022/01/tsedal-neeley-on-why-we-need-to-think-of-the-office-as-a-tool-with-very-specific-uses

New York Times. (2021, October 15). *Covid in Italy: Protests fizzle as government imposes vaccine mandate in workplaces*. https://www.nytimes.com/live/2021/10/15/world/italy-covid-green-pass

Newman, A. (2021, December 29). *New York City is being pummeled by Omicron*. The New York Times. https://www.nytimes.com/live/2021/12/29/world/omicron-covid-vaccine-tests/new-york-city-is-being-pummeled-by-omicron

Newport, C. (2019). *Digital minimalism: Choosing a focused life in a noisy world*. Portfolio.

Newport, C. (2021). *A world without email: Reimagining work in an age of communication overload*. Portfolio.

Nguyen, L. (2022, January 7). *Citigroup prepares to fire unvaccinated employees at the end of January*. The New York Times. https://www.nytimes.com/2022/01/07/business/citigroup-vaccine-mandate.html

Niccol, A. (2011). *In time*. Twentieth Century Fox.

Nohria, N., & Khurana, R. (Eds.). (2010). *Handbook of leadership and practice: An Harvard Business School centennial colloquium on advancing leadership*. Harvard Business Press.

Nooyi, I. (2021, November 5). *Indra Nooyi, former CEO of PepsiCo, on nurturing talent in turbulent times*. Harvard Business Review. https://hbr.org/video/6280323377001/indra-nooyi-former-ceo-of-pepsico-on-nurturing-talent-in-turbulent-times

O'Connor, C., & Weatherall, J. O. (2019). *The misinformation age: How false beliefs spread* (1st ed.). Yale University Press.

O'Neil, S. (2021). *Be where your feet are: Seven principles to keep you present, grounded, and thriving*. Macmillan Audio.

Obama, B. (2008, August 28). *Transcript: Barack Obama's acceptance speech*. National Public Radio (NPR). https://www.npr.org/templates/story/story.php?storyId=94087570

Office for Civil Rights (OCR) - U.S. Department of Health & Human Services. (2020, November 2). *Employers and health information in the workplace*. https://www.hhs.gov/hipaa/for-individuals/employers-health-information-workplace/index.html

Olmstead v. United States, 277 U.S. 438, (1928).

Olson, T., & Singman, B. (2021, December 30). *Congressional Republicans tell Supreme Court to block Biden's "health police" vaccine mandate*. Fox News Network. https://www.foxnews.com/politics/supreme-court-stefanik-braun-covid-vaccine-mandate

Onyeaka, H., Anumudu, C. K., Al-Sharify, Z. T., Egele-Godswill, E., & Mbaegbu, P. (2021). COVID-19 pandemic: A review of the global lockdown and its far-reaching effects. *Science Progress, 104*(2),

003685042110198. https://doi.org/10.1177/00368504211019854

Origgi, G. (2017). *Reputation: What it is and why it matters.* Princeton University Press.

Otterman, S. (2020, December 14). *'I trust science,' says nurse who is first to get vaccine in U.S.* The New York Times. https://www.nytimes.com/2020/12/14/nyregion/us-covid-vaccine-first-sandra-lindsay.html

Otterman, S., & Goldstein, J. (2022, January 7). *More patients, fewer workers: Omicron pushes New York hospitals to brink.* The New York Times. https://www.nytimes.com/2022/01/07/nyregion/ny-hospitals-omicron-covid.html

Pace, M. (2015). *Dark psychology 101: Learn the secrets of covert emotional manipulation, dark persuasion, undetected mind control, mind games, deception, hypnotism, brainwashing and other tricks of the trade.* Make Profits Easy.

Padilla, M. (2019, November 21). *Virus outbreak closes Colorado schools for more than 20,000 students.* The New York Times. https://www.nytimes.com/2019/11/21/us/virus-colorado-schools-close.html

Pappas, S. (2020, October 1). The toll of job loss: The unemployment and economic crises sparked by COVID-19 are expected to have far-reaching mental health impacts. *Monitor on Psychology, 51*(7), 54. https://www.apa.org/monitor/2020/10/toll-job-loss

Parker-Pope, T., Caron, C., & Sancho, M. C. (2021, December 17). *Why 1,320 therapists are worried about mental health in America right now.* The New York Times. https://www.nytimes.com/interactive/2021/12/16/well/mental-health-crisis-america-covid.html

Parmet, W. (2022, January 6). *The government's ability to control the pandemic is at stake.* The New York Times. https://www.nytimes.com/2022/01/06/opinion/supreme-court-vaccine-mandates.html

Patten, E. (2016, July 1). *Racial, gender wage gaps persist in U.S. despite some progress.* Pew Research. https://www.pewresearch.org/fact-tank/2016/07/01/racial-gender-wage-gaps-persist-in-u-s-despite-some-progress/

Paul, M. (2021, December 20). *Another layer of torment: 'COVID shame.'*

Northwestern University. https://news.northwestern.edu/stories/2021/12/covid-shame-torments-the-infected/#:~:text=As if contracting COVID-19,patients can cope with it.

Paybarah, A., & Abelson, R. (2021, November 30). *A federal judge blocks Biden's vaccine mandate for U.S. health workers.* The New York Times. https://www.nytimes.com/2021/11/30/world/vaccine-mandate-health-workers-blocked.html

Pearn, M., & Mulrooney, C. (2017). *Ending the blame culture* (1st ed.). Routledge.

Peloza, J., Loock, M., Cerruti, J., & Muyot, M. (2012). Sustainability: How stakeholder perceptions differ from corporate reality. *California Management Review, 55*(1). https://doi.org/10.1525/cmr.2012.55.1.74

Pentaris, P. (Ed.). (2021). *Death, grief and loss in the context of COVID-19* (1st ed.). Routledge.

Peter H. Kahn, J., & Thea Weiss. (2017). The importance of children interacting with Big Nature. *Children, Youth and Environments, 27*(2), 7–24. https://doi.org/10.7721/chilyoutenvi.27.2.0007

Pierce, R. (2020, June 19). *Are you suffering from shifting baseline syndrome?* Earth. https://earth.org/shifting-baseline-syndrome/

Pietrangelo, A. (2020, June 16). *The impacts of the glass ceiling effect on people.* Healthline. https://www.healthline.com/health/mental-health/glass-ceiling-effect

Piezunka, H., Aggarwal, V. A., & Posen, H. E. (2021, October 5). *What to do with contrarians?* Insead Knowledge. https://knowledge.insead.edu/entrepreneurship/what-to-do-with-contrarians-17461

Piketty, T. (2020). *Capital and ideology.* Harvard University Press.

Pildes, R. H. (2021, December 29). *Why so many Democracies are floundering.* The New York Times. https://www.nytimes.com/2021/12/29/opinion/democracy-fragmentation-america-europe.html

Pisani, N. (2021, May 13). *How COVID-19 will change the geography of competition.* MIT Salon Management Review. https://sloanreview.mit.edu/article/how-covid-19-will-change-the-geography-of-competition/

Place, A. (2021, November 22). *Unvaccinated employees are lying about their status to retain their jobs*. Employee Benefit News (EBN). https://www.benefitnews.com/news/unvaccinated-employees-are-lying-about-their-status-to-retain-their-jobs

Porter, M. E. (2011). *The competitive advantage of nations: Creating and sustaining superior performance*. Free Press.

Price, D. (2021). *Laziness does not exist*. Atria Books.

Pruitt, S. (2019, March 26). *How "duck-and-cover" drills channeled America's Cold War anxiety*. History. https://www.history.com/news/duck-cover-drills-cold-war-arms-race#:~:text=By the early 1950s%2C schools,over an escalating arms race.

Qualtrics. (2021, November 18). *Research: Nearly 30% of unvaccinated workers would consider lying about their vaccination status*. Qualtrics.Com. https://www.qualtrics.com/blog/lie-about-being-vaccinated/

Ratcliffe, S., & Wilson, J. (2021, September 24). *Work can be better post-COVID-19. Here's what employers need to know*. World Economic Forum. https://www.weforum.org/agenda/2021/09/work-can-be-better-post-covid-heres-how/

Reel Black. (2021, June 26). *Dick Gregory: Complete truth (2015/2021)|Remastered| w 7 minutes of previously unseen material*. Youtube. https://www.youtube.com/watch?v=lIoKiVdHdpc

Rego, M. (2021, December 8). *Why is mental pain considered less important than physical pain?* Psychology Today. https://www.psychologytoday.com/us/blog/modern-world-modern-mind/202112/why-is-mental-pain-considered-less-important-physical-pain

Reich, R. B. (2020). *The system: Who rigged it, how we fix it*. Vintage.

Reisinger, H., & Fetterer, D. (2021, October 29). *Forget flexibility. Your employees want autonomy*. Harvard Business Review. https://hbr.org/2021/10/forget-flexibility-your-employees-want-autonomy?ab=hero-main-text

Repucci, S., & Slipowitz, A. (2021). Freedom in the world 2021: Democracy under siege. In *Freedom House*.

Ressler, C., & Thompson, J. (2015). *Why work sucks and how to fix it: The results-only revolution.* CultureRx.

Reuters. (2020, October 13). *Biggest WWII bomb explodes underwater in Poland during deactivation.* https://www.dailysabah.com/world/europe/biggest-wwii-bomb-explodes-underwater-in-poland-during-deactivation

Reuters. (2021, December 1). *Four injured after old WWII aircraft bomb explodes in Munich - police.* https://www.reuters.com/world/europe/three-injured-after-explosion-munich-police-2021-12-01/

Reuters. (2022, January 2). *Dutch police disperse anti-lockdown protesters in Amsterdam.* https://www.reuters.com/business/media-telecom/dutch-police-disperse-thousands-protesting-against-lockdown-measures-2022-01-02/

Rice, C. (2011). *No higher honor: A memoir of my years in Washington* (1st ed.). Crown.

Richardson, E. (2003). "R-E-S-P-E-C-T." *O, The Oprah Magazine, 4*(4), 196.

Rid, T. (2020). *Active measures: The secret history of disinformation and political warfare* (Illustrate). Farrar, Straus and Giroux.

Ridley, M. (2020, May 29). So where did the virus come from? *Dow Jones Institutional News.* https://www.wsj.com/articles/so-where-did-the-virus-come-from-11590756909

Ridley, M., & Chan, A. (2021). *Viral: The search for the origin of COVID-19.* Harper.

Robbins, R., & Jewett, C. (2021, December 16). *C.D.C. recommends other Covid vaccines over J.&J.'s shots.* The New York Times. https://www.nytimes.com/2021/12/16/health/johnson-and-johnson-vaccine-blood-clots.html

Roberts, M. (2021, October 28). *Covid: Double vaccinated can still spread virus at home.* British Broadcasting Corporation (BBC). https://www.bbc.com/news/health-59077036

Robinson, B. E. (2014). *Chained to the desk: A guidebook for workaholics, their partners and children, and the clinicians who treat them* (3rd ed.). NYU Press.

Rock, D., & Pruitt-Haynes, C. (2021, September 23). *Why mandates make us feel threatened.* Harvard Business Review. https://hbr.org/2021/09/why-mandates-make-us-feel-threatened

Ronningstam, E. (2014). Narcissistic Personality Disorder. In *Gabbard's Treatments of Psychiatric Disorders*. American Psychiatric Publishing. https://doi.org/10.1176/appi.books.9781585625048.gg72

Rosenblum, N. L., & Muirhead, R. (2020). *A lot of people are saying: The new conspiracism and the assault on democracy.* Princeton University Press.

Rosenzweig, P. (2007). *The halo effect: ... and the eight other business delusions that deceive managers* (Reissue). Free Press.

Ross, L., Greene, D., & House, P. (1977). The "false consensus effect": An egocentric bias in social perception and attribution processes. *Journal of Experimental Social Psychology, 13*(3), 279–301. https://doi.org/10.1016/0022-1031(77)90049-X

Rowan, L. (2021, November 4). *Fired for not following Biden's vaccine mandate? It's unlikely you'll get unemployment.* Forbes. https://www.forbes.com/advisor/personal-finance/biden-vaccine-mandate-unemployment-eligibility/

Ruane, M. E. (2020, April 14). *The tainted polio vaccine that sickened and fatally paralyzed children in 1955.* The Washington Post. https://www.washingtonpost.com/history/2020/04/14/cutter-polio-vaccine-paralyzed-children-coronavirus/

Rudolph, C. W., & Zacher, H. (2021). Employee well-being in the face of a pandemic: Organizational and managerial responses to COVID-19. In *Society for Industrial and Organizational Psychology (SIOP).* https://www.siop.org/Portals/84/docs/White Papers/Visibility/PostCOVID.pdf?ver=P6APUAAH5XKh6f1cg5sFLA%3D%3D

Russo, J. E., & Schoemaker, P. J. H. (1989). *Decision traps: The ten barriers to brilliant decision-making and how to overcome them.* Simon & Schuster.

Rutherford, A. (2019). *Learn to think in systems: Use system archetypes to understand, manage, and fix complex problems and make smarter decisions.* Kindle Direct Publishing.

Rutschman, A. S. (2021, November 18). *Why Moderna won't share rights to the COVID-19 vaccine with the government that paid for its development.* The Conversation. https://theconversation.com/why-moderna-wont-share-rights-to-the-covid-19-vaccine-with-the-government-that-paid-for-its-development-172008

Ryzhkov, V. (2011, April 11). *Soviet tyranny was a crime against humanity.* The Moscow Times. https://www.themoscowtimes.com/2011/04/11/soviet-tyranny-was-a-crime-against-humanity-a6252

Saad, G. (2020). *The parasitic mind: How infectious ideas are killing common sense.* Regnery Publishing.

Sachs, D. (2020, October 26). *Denver City Council spikes $25 million contract with private security company Allied Universal.* Dinverite. https://denverite.com/2020/10/26/denver-city-council-spikes-25-million-contract-with-private-security-company-allied-universal/

Santoro, H. (2021, November). The science of uncertainty. *Monitor on Psychology, 52*(8). https://www.apa.org/monitor/2021/11/lab-science-uncertainty

Sarasohn, E. (2021, October 5). *The great executive-employee disconnect.* Future Forum. https://futureforum.com/2021/10/05/the-great-executive-employee-disconnect/

Sargant, W., & Swencionis, C. (2019). *Battle for the mind: A physiology of conversion and brainwashing - How evangelists, psychiatrists, politicians, and medicine men can change your beliefs and behavior.* Prabhat Prakashan.

Scarry, E. (2012). *Thinking in an emergency* (Reprint). W. W. Norton & Company.

Schnell, M. (2021, November 17). *OSHA suspends enforcement of COVID-19 vaccine mandate for businesses.* The Hill. https://thehill.com/policy/healthcare/582022-osha-suspends-enforcement-of-covid-19-vaccine-mandate-for-businesses

Schön, D. A. (2017). *The reflective practitioner: How professionals think in action.* Routledge.

Schonfeld, I. S., Cigularov, K., & Chang, C.-H. (2017). *Occupational health psychology* (1st ed.). Springer Publishing Company.

Schuetze, C. F. (2021a, December 2). *Germany announces tough restrictions for unvaccinated people.* The New York Times. https://www.nytimes.com/2021/12/02/world/europe/germany-coronavirus.html

Schuetze, C. F. (2021b, December 2). *Germany shuts unvaccinated people out of much of public life.* The New York Times. https://www.nytimes.com/2021/12/02/world/europe/germany-unvaccinated-restrictions.html

Schwartz, T., (with Gomes, J., & (with McCarthy, C. (2010). *The way we're working isn't working: The four forgotten needs that energize great performance.* Free Press.

Scott, J. C. (2020). *Seeing like a state: How certain schemes to improve the human condition have failed.* Yale University Press.

Selznick, P., & Simon, J. (2011). *TVA and the grass roots: A study of politics and organization.* Quid Pro Books.

Senatori, I., & Spinelli, C. (2021). (Re-)regulating remote work in the post-pandemic scenario: Lessons from the Italian experience. *Italian Labour Law E-Journal,* 14(1), 209–260. https://doi.org/10.6092/issn.1561-8048/13376

Senge, P. (2010). *The fifth discipline: The art & practice of the learning organization* (Revised & Updated). Currency.

Seymour, R. (2020). *The Twittering Machine.* Verso.

Shambaugh, R. (2007). *It's not a glass ceiling, it's a sticky floor: Free yourself from the hidden behaviors sabotaging your career success* (1st ed.). McGraw-Hill Education.

Shambi, J. (2021, November 10). *Rethinking experience|Supporting women in a work from home world.* LIGS University. https://www.ligsuniversity.com/en/blogpost/rethinking-experience-supporting-women-in-a-work-from-home-world?utm_content=bufferdd7ab&utm_medium=social&utm_source=linkedin.com&utm_campaign=buffer

Shaner, D. (2010). *The seven arts of change: Leading business transformation that lasts.* Union Square Press.

Sherfinski, D. (2021, December 16). *Analysis: Jabs for jobs: U.S. vaccine mandates offer bargaining chip for worker rights.* Reuters. https://www.reuters.com/world/us/jabs-jobs-us-vaccine-mandates-offer-bargaining-chip-worker-rights-2021-12-16/

Shirer, W. L. (2011). *The rise and fall of the Third Reich.* RosettaBooks.

Silbiger, S. (2012). *The ten-day MBA: A step-by-step guide to mastering the skills taught in America's top business schools* (4th ed.). HarperCollins.

Simons, A. (2020, June 8). *Managing remote terminations during COVID-19.* Control Risk. https://www.controlrisks.com/our-thinking/insights/managing-remote-terminations-during-covid-19

Sinek, S. (2019). *The infinite game.* Portfolio/Penguin.

Singanayagam, A., Hakki, S., Dunning, J., Madon, K. J., Crone, M. A., Koycheva, A., Derqui-Fernandez, N., Barnett, J. L., Whitfield, M. G., Varro, R., Charlett, A., Kundu, R., Fenn, J., Cutajar, J., Quinn, V., Conibear, E., Barclay, W., Freemont, P. S., Taylor, G. P., ... Lackenby, A. (2021). Community transmission and viral load kinetics of the SARS-CoV-2 delta (B.1.617.2) variant in vaccinated and unvaccinated individuals in the UK: a prospective, longitudinal, cohort study. *The Lancet Infectious Diseases.* https://doi.org/10.1016/S1473-3099(21)00648-4

Singer, P. (2019). *The life you can save: How to do your part to end world poverty* (10th Anniversary). Life You Can Save.

Slater, P. (2016). *The pursuit of loneliness: America's discontent and the search for a new Democratic ideal: Twentieth anniversary edition* (3rd ed.). Beacon Press.

Slotnik, D. E. (2021, October 4). *New York's largest health care provider fires 1,400 unvaccinated employees.* The New York Times. https://www.nytimes.com/2021/10/04/nyregion/northwell-employees-fired.html

Smart, S., & Ravindran, J. (2021, December 31). *Chicago woman quarantined in airplane bathroom for 3 hours after testing positive for Covid-19 mid-flight.* Cable News Network (CNN). https://www.cnn.com/travel/article/icelandair-covid-passenger-quarantines-trnd/index.html

Smialek, J. (2022, January 12). *Consumer prices popped again in December as policymakers await an elusive peak.* The New York Times. https://www.nytimes.com/2022/01/12/business/economy/cpi-inflation-december-2021.html

Smith, A. (2021, September 29). *Firing unvaccinated workers becomes more common.* Society for Human Resource Management (SHRM). https://www.shrm.org/resourcesandtools/legal-and-compliance/employment-law/pages/coronavirus-firing-unvaccinated-workers.aspx

Smith, A., & Nagele-Piazza, L. (2021, November 1). *Employers react to workers who refuse a COVID-19 vaccination.* Society for Human Resource Management (SHRM). https://www.shrm.org/resourcesandtools/legal-and-compliance/employment-law/pages/if-workers-refuse-a-covid-19-vaccination.aspx

Smith, L. (2010). *Psychology, poverty, and the end of social exclusion: Putting our practice to work* (58120th ed.). Teachers College Press.

Smith, N. C., Scholz, M., & Williams, J. (2021, December 2). Does your business need a human rights strategy? *MIT Salon Management Review, 63*(2), 64–72. https://sloanreview.mit.edu/article/does-your-business-need-a-human-rights-strategy/

Smith, W., & Manson, M. (2021). *Will.* Penguin Press.

Sneed, T. (2021a, December 18). *Appeals court lets Biden administration enforce vaccine rules for large employers.* Cable News Network (CNN). https://www.cnn.com/2021/12/17/politics/appeals-court-vaccine-mandate-osha-large-employers-federal-contractors/index.html

Sneed, T. (2021b, December 29). *The Supreme Court has upheld state and local vaccine mandates. That may not save Biden's.* Cable News Network (CNN). https://www.cnn.com/2021/12/29/politics/supreme-court-vaccine-mandates-federal-biden/index.html

Sommer, J. (2002, February 17). *Retirements delayed by losses, survey says.* The New York Times. https://www.nytimes.com/2002/02/17/business/yourmoney/retirements-delayed-by-losses-survey-says.html?searchResultPosition=24

Sowell, T. (2009). *Applied economics: Thinking beyond stage one: Revised and enlarged edition.* Basic Books.

Sperling, G. B. (2020). *Economic dignity.* Penguin Press.

Spitz, V. (2005). *Doctors from hell: The horrific account of Nazi experiments on humans* (1st ed.). Sentient Publications.

Spranca, M., Minsk, E., & Baron, J. (1991). Omission and commission in judgment and choice. *Journal of Experimental Social Psychology, 27*(1), 76–105. https://doi.org/10.1016/0022-1031(91)90011-T

Springer Nature. (2020, April 22). *Coronavirus: The first three months as it happened*. Nature. https://doi.org/10.1038/d41586-020-00154-w

State of Louisiana et al. v. Xavier Becerra et al. Case No. 3:21-Cv-03970, (2021).

State of Missouri et al. v. Joseph R. Biden, Jr., in his official capacity as the President of the United States of America et al. Case No. 4:21-cv-01329-MTS, (2021).

Stephens, B. (2021, November 30). *Let's end the Covid blame games*. The New York Times.

Stern, R. (2007). *The gaslight effect: How to spot and survive the hidden manipulation others use to control your life*. Harmony.

Stever, G. S., Giles, D. C., Cohen, J. D., & Myers, M. E. (2021). *Understanding media psychology* (1st ed.). Routledge.

Stout, M. (2020). *Outsmarting the sociopath next door: How to protect yourself against a ruthless manipulator*. Harmony.

Strauss, W., & Howe, N. (2009). *The fourth turning: What the cycles of history tell us about America's next rendezvous with destiny* (Reprint). Crown.

Stroud, R. (2021, November 18). *Bucs' Antonio Brown accused of obtaining fake vaccine card*. Tampa Bay Times. https://www.tampabay.com/sports/bucs/2021/11/18/bucs-antonio-brown-accused-of-obtaining-fake-vaccine-card/

Sull, D., Sull, C., & Zweig, B. (2022, January 11). *Toxic culture is driving the Great Resignation*. MIT Sloan Management Review. https://sloanreview.mit.edu/article/toxic-culture-is-driving-the-great-resignation/

Sullivan, B. (2019). *Pleased to meet me: Genes, germs, and the curious forces that make us who we are*. Blackstone Audio.

Summers, J. (2020, October 2). *Timeline: How Trump has downplayed the Coronavirus Pandemic*. National Public Radio (NPR). https://www.npr.org/sections/latest-updates-trump-covid-19-results/2020/10/02/919432383/how-trump-has-downplayed-the-coronavirus-pandemic

Sun, H.-Y., Li, A.-M., Chen, S., Zhao, D., Rao, L.-L., Liang, Z.-Y., & Li, S. (2015). Pain now or later: An outgrowth account of pain-minimization. *PLOS ONE, 10*(3), e0119320.

https://doi.org/10.1371/journal.pone.0119320

Susarla, A., Kim, D. H., & Zuckerman, E. (2021, December 27). *What will 2022 bring in the way of misinformation on social media? 3 experts weigh in.* The Conversation. https://theconversation.com/what-will-2022-bring-in-the-way-of-misinformation-on-social-media-3-experts-weigh-in-173952

Sutton, R. I. (2007). *The no asshole rule: Building a civilized workplace and surviving one that isn't* (1st ed.). Business Plus.

Sweeny, K., & Andrews, S. E. (2014). Mapping individual differences in the experience of a waiting period. *Journal of Personality and Social Psychology, 106*(6), 1015–1030. https://doi.org/10.1037/a0036031

Sweeny, K., Carroll, P. J., & Shepperd, J. A. (2006). Is optimism always best?: Future outlooks and preparedness. *Current Directions in Psychological Science, 15*(6), 302–306. https://doi.org/10.1111/j.1467-8721.2006.00457.x

Sweeny, K., & Shepperd, J. A. (2007a). Do people brace sensibly? Risk judgments and event likelihood. *Personality and Social Psychology Bulletin,* 33(8), 1064–1075. https://doi.org/10.1177/0146167207301024

Sweeny, K., & Shepperd, J. A. (2007b). Being the best bearer of bad tidings. *Review of General Psychology, 11*(3), 235–257. https://doi.org/10.1037/1089-2680.11.3.235

Syal, A. (2021, November 17). *Hospitalizations rising among fully vaccinated in U.S., Fauci says.* CNBC. https://www.nbcnews.com/health/health-news/hospitalizations-rising-fully-vaccinated-us-fauci-says-rcna5907

Szekely, F., Dossa, Z., & Hollender, J. (2017). *Beyond the triple bottom line: Eight steps toward a sustainable business model.* MIT Press.

Taleb, N. N. (2010). *The black swan: The impact of the highly improbable* (2nd ed.). Random House.

Tanner, L. (2021, December 28). *First COVID-19 shot recipient in US now a vaccine activist.* The Associated Press. https://apnews.com/article/coronavirus-pandemic-science-health-united-states-8109a5047212947ab3a1f27dac8ec099

Tanusree, J., & Brennan, L. (2021, November 16). *What space missions can teach us about remote work.* MIT Salon Management Review.

Tavernise, S. (2021, December 26). First they fought about masks. Then over the soul of the city. *The New York Times*, A1. https://www.nytimes.com/2021/12/26/us/oklahoma-masks.html?searchResultPosition=2

Tayag, Y. (2021, November 8). *How easily can vaccinated people spread COVID?* The Atlantic. https://www.theatlantic.com/science/archive/2021/11/vaccinated-spread-the-coronavirus/620650/

Taylor, F. W. (2009). *The principles of scientific management.* Digireads.com.

Taylor, K. (2017). *Brainwashing: The science of thought control* (2nd ed.). Oxford University Press.

Taylor, S. (2021). *The psychology of pandemics: Preparing for the next global outbreak of infectious disease.* William James Ransom.

Taylor, T. (2020). *A CEO only does three Things: finding your focus in the C-Suite.* A Board of Advisors Book.

Tedeschi, R. G., Moore, B. A., (with Falke, K., & (with Goldberg, J. (2020). *Transformed by trauma: Stories of posttraumatic growth.* Boulder Crest.

Tercatin, R. (2021, December 1). *COVID: Time for Israel to consider vaccine mandate – commissioner.* The Jerusalem Post. https://www.jpost.com/health-and-wellness/coronavirus/covid-time-for-israel-to-consider-vaccine-mandate-commissioner-687507

Thaler, R. (1980). Toward a positive theory of consumer choice. *Journal of Economic Behavior & Organization, 1*(1), 39–60. https://doi.org/10.1016/0167-2681(80)90051-7

Thaler, R. H., & Sunstein, C. R. (2021). *Nudge: The final edition.* Penguin Books.

The Holy Bible, New King James Version. (1982). Thomas Nelson.

The State of Georgia, et al., v. Joseph R. Biden, in his official capacity as President of the United States, et al. CIVIL ACTION NO.: 1:21-cv-163, (2021).

Thomas, W., Hujala, A., Laulainen, S., & McMurray, R. (Eds.). (2018). *The management of wicked problems in health and social care* (1st ed.). Routledge.

Thomson, J. J. (1976). Killing, letting die, and the Trolley problem. *The Monist, 59*(2), 204–217.

Towey, H. (2021, December 6). *Better.com CEO accused hundreds of the 900 people he laid off on Zoom of "stealing" by working only 2 hours daily.* Yahoo Money. https://money.yahoo.com/better-com-ceo-accused-hundreds-161831980.html

Treisman, R. (2021, December 6). *Over a dozen COVID cases were found on a cruise ship that just docked in New Orleans.* National Public Radio (NPR). https://www.npr.org/2021/12/06/1061799633/norwegian-cruise-lines-covid-outbreak-new-orleans-omicron

Trout, J., & (with Rivkin, S. (2015). *Differentiate or die: Survival in our era of killer competition* (2nd ed.). Westland.

Tuerck, D. D. (2021). *Macroeconomics* (3rd ed.). Business Expert Press.

Tyson, B., Fareed, G., & (with Crawford, M. (2022). *Overcoming the COVID-19 darkness: How two doctors successfully treated 7000 patients.* Brian Tyson, M.D. and George C. Fareed, M.D.

U.S. Centers for Disease Control and Prevention (CDC). (2021a, June 7). *CDC COVID-19 study shows mRNA vaccines reduce risk of infection by 91 percent for fully vaccinated people.* https://www.cdc.gov/media/releases/2021/p0607-mrna-reduce-risks.html

U.S. Centers for Disease Control and Prevention (CDC). (2021b, November 9). *The possibility of COVID-19 after vaccination: Breakthrough infections.* https://www.cdc.gov/coronavirus/2019-ncov/vaccines/effectiveness/why-measure-effectiveness/breakthrough-cases.html

U.S. Centers for Disease Control and Prevention (CDC). (2021c, November 29). *CDC expands COVID-19 booster recommendations.* https://www.cdc.gov/media/releases/2021/s1129-booster-recommendations.html

U.S. Centers for Disease Control and Prevention (CDC). (2021d, December 23). *Interim clinical considerations for use of COVID-19 vaccines currently approved or authorized in the United States.* https://www.cdc.gov/vaccines/covid-19/clinical-considerations/covid-19-vaccines-us.html

U.S. Centers for Disease Control and Prevention (CDC). (2021e, December 30). *COVID-19 and cruise ship travel.*

https://wwwnc.cdc.gov/travel/notices/covid-4/coronavirus-cruise-ship

U.S. Department of Transportation - Federal Aviation Administration. (2022a, January 11). *2021 unruly passenger data.* https://www.faa.gov/data_research/passengers_cargo/unruly_passengers/2021_archive/

U.S. Department of Transportation - Federal Aviation Administration. (2022b, January 12). *Unruly passengers.* https://www.faa.gov/data_research/passengers_cargo/unruly_passengers/

U.S. Equal Employment Opportunity Commission. (2002, October 17). *Enforcement guidance on reasonable accommodation and undue hardship under the ADA.* U.S. Equal Employment Opportunity Commission. https://www.eeoc.gov/laws/guidance/enforcement-guidance-reasonable-accommodation-and-undue-hardship-under-ada

U.S. Equal Employment Opportunity Commission. (2021, May 28). *What you should know about COVID-19 and the ADA, the Rehabilitation Act, and other EEO laws.* https://www.eeoc.gov/wysk/what-you-should-know-about-covid-19-and-ada-rehabilitation-act-and-other-eeo-laws

U.S. Food and Drug Administration. (2021, August 23). *FDA approves first COVID-19 vaccine.* https://www.fda.gov/news-events/press-announcements/fda-approves-first-covid-19-vaccine#:~:text=Today%2C the U.S. Food and,years of age and older.

U.S. Navy Seals 1-26, et al. v. Joseph R. Biden, Jr., et al. No. 4:21-cv-01236-O, (2022).

U.S. Social Security Administration (SSA). (2021). *How you earn credits.* https://www.ssa.gov/pubs/EN-05-10072.pdf

Ulrich, D., Zenger, J., Smallwood, N., & Bennis, W. (1999). *Results-based leadership: How leaders build the business and improve the bottom line.* Harvard Business School Press.

United Nations. (1965, December 21). *International convention on the elimination of all forms of racial discrimination.* United Nations. https://www.ohchr.org/en/professionalinterest/pages/cerd.aspx

United Nations. (2018, April 20). *Do you know all 17 SDGs?* Youtube. https://www.youtube.com/watch?v=0XTBYMfZyrM&t=6s

United States v. Peters, 9 U.S. 115, (1809).

University of California Television (UCTV). (2017, September 6). *The hacking of the American mind with Dr. Robert Lustig.* Youtube. https://www.youtube.com/watch?v=EKkUtrL6B18&t=1215s

University of Pittsburgh Medical Center (UPMC). (2021, July 26). *Researchers identify groups hesitant about COVID-19 vaccine.* https://www.upmc.com/media/news/072621-king-mejia-vaccine-hesitancy

University of Southampton. (2021, July 6). *Study shows laboratory developed protein spikes consistent with COVID-19 virus.* ScienceDaily. Study shows laboratory developed protein spikes consistent with COVID-19 virus. ScienceDaily

University of Washington. (2017, November 15). *What counts as "nature"? It all depends.* ScienceDaily. https://www.sciencedaily.com/releases/2017/11/171115124514.htm

Vakil, C. (2021a, October 29). *Vaccinated just as likely to spread delta variant within household as unvaccinated: study.* The Hill. https://thehill.com/policy/healthcare/579068-vaccinated-just-as-likely-to-spread-delta-variant-as-unvaccinated-study

Vakil, C. (2021b, December 2). *Nevada to make unvaccinated state workers pay insurance surcharge.* The Hill. https://thehill.com/homenews/state-watch/584168-nevada-to-make-unvaccinated-state-workers-pay-insurance-surcharge

Valinsky, J. (2021, November 8). *Aaron Rodgers' State Farm commercials are disappearing from your TV.* Cable News Network (CNN). https://www.cnn.com/2021/11/08/media/aaron-rodgers-state-farm-sponsorship/index.html

Van Horn, C. E. (2014). *Working scared (or not at all): The lost decade, great recession, and restoring the shattered American Dream* (Updated). Rowman & Littlefield Publishers.

van Prooijen, J.-W., & Krouwel, A. P. M. (2019). Psychological features of extreme political ideologies. *Current Directions in Psychological Science, 28*(2), 159–163. https://doi.org/10.1177/0963721418817755

Vanderbloemen, W. (2018). *Culture wins: The roadmap to an irresistible workplace.* Savio Republic.

Vijayakumar, C. (2021, January 14). *Workplace disrupted – five themes that will define the future of work.* World Economic Forum. https://www.weforum.org/agenda/2021/01/5-themes-that-will-define-the-future-of-work/

Vitka, W. (2021, October 1). *DC Council member questions religious exemption for COVID vaccines.* WTOP. https://wtop.com/dc/2021/10/dc-council-member-questions-religious-exemption-for-covid-vaccines/

Wachowski, L., & Wachowski, L. (1999). *The Matrix.* Warner Bros.

WAFB Staff. (2021, October 3). *Ochsner puts pressure on employees' spouses to get COVID-19 vaccine or health care fees could rise.* Fox 8. https://www.fox8live.com/2021/10/04/ochsner-puts-pressure-employees-spouses-get-covid-19-vaccine-or-health-care-fees-could-rise/

Wallisch, P. (2014, November 17). *Psychopaths in our midst — what you should know.* Elsevier. https://www.elsevier.com/connect/psychopaths-what-are-they-and-how-should-we-deal-with-them

Wamsley, L. (2021, March 11). *March 11, 2020: The day everything changed.* National Public Radio (NPR). https://www.npr.org/2021/03/11/975663437/march-11-2020-the-day-everything-changed

Ware, B. (2019). *Top five regrets of the dying: A life transformed by the dearly departing.* Hay House.

Washington Post Live. (2021, September 24). *Transcript: The Great Resignation with Molly M. Anderson, Anthony C. Klotz, PhD & Elaine Welteroth.* The Washington Post. https://www.washingtonpost.com/washington-post-live/2021/09/24/transcript-great-resignation-with-molly-m-anderson-anthony-c-klotz-phd-elaine-welteroth/

Wegner, D. M. (1989). *White bears and other unwanted thoughts: Suppression, obsession, and the psychology of mental control.* Viking. https://archive.org/details/whitebearsotheru0000wegn_j1l7

Weisinger, H., & Pawliw-Fry, J. P. (2015). *Performing under pressure: The science of doing your best when it matters most.* Currency.

Weisman, J. (2021, November 24). *G.O.P. fights covid mandates, then blames Biden as cases rise.* The New York Times. https://www.nytimes.com/2021/11/24/us/politics/republicans-biden-coronavirus.html?

Weitz, J. S., Park, S. W., Eksin, C., & Dushoff, J. (2020). Awareness-driven behavior changes can shift the shape of epidemics away from peaks and toward plateaus, shoulders, and oscillations. *Proceedings of the National Academy of Sciences, 117*(51), 32764–32771. https://doi.org/10.1073/pnas.2009911117

Westerman, G. (2021, October 28). *Rethinking assumptions about how employees work.* MIT Salon Management Review. https://sloanreview.mit.edu/article/rethinking-assumptions-about-how-employees-work/

Wetrich, J. G. (2021). *Stifled: Where good leaders go wrong.* Leaders Press.

Whelan, R., & Evans, M. (2021, December 13). *Some hospitals drop Covid-19 vaccine mandates to ease labor shortages.* The Wall Street Journal. https://www.wsj.com/articles/some-hospitals-drop-covid-19-vaccine-mandates-to-ease-labor-shortages-11639396806

Whillans, A., Feldman, D., & Wisniewski, D. (2021, November 12). *The psychology behind meeting overload.* Harvard Business Review. https://hbr.org/2021/11/the-psychology-behind-meeting-overload?ab=hero-main-text

White House. (2021, December 21). *President Biden delivers remarks on the status of the country's fight against COVID-19.* Youtube. https://www.youtube.com/watch?v=95NfeWiJfRs

Whitney, B. (2021, November 18). *Phoenix-area companies advertising "no vaccine required" on job applications.* AZFamily.Com. https://www.azfamily.com/news/continuing_coverage/coronavirus_coverage/vaccine_headquarters/no-vaccine-required-at-some-jobs/article_717dd924-48e1-11ec-a283-6bc57af39e08.html

Wilkerson, I. (2020). *Caste: The origins of our discontents.* Random House.

Wilkerson, I. (2021, June 16). Live chat: Caste with Isabel Wilkerson. *Task Force on Racism, IFC Corporate Strategy & Resources Vice Presidency and East Asian Women's Network.*

Winn, D. (2011). *The manipulated mind.* Malor Books.

Wolff, M. (2021). *Landslide: The final days of the Trump Presidency.* Henry Holt and Co.

Wolff, R. D. (2021). *The sickness is the system: When capitalism fails to save us from pandemics or itself*. Democracy at Work.

Wolpe, P. R. (2013). *Explaining social deviance*. Great Courses.

Wood, E. M. (2016). *The origin of capitalism: A longer view* (Revised). Verso.

Woodard, C. (2016). *American character: A history of the epic struggle between individual liberty and the common good*. Penguin Books.

World Health Organization (WHO). (2021a, August 27). *Moving towards digital documentation of COVID-19 status.* https://www.who.int/news/item/27-08-2021-moving-towards-digital-documentation-of-covid-19-status

World Health Organization (WHO). (2021b, November 28). *Enhancing readiness for Omicron (B.1.1.529): Technical brief and priority actions for member states.* https://www.who.int/publications/m/item/enhancing-readiness-for-omicron-(b.1.1.529)-technical-brief-and-priority-actions-for-member-states

Wright, A. D. (2017, August 7). *Microchipping employees: Do the pros outweigh the cons?* Society for Human Resource Management (SHRM). https://www.shrm.org/resourcesandtools/hr-topics/technology/pages/microchipping-employees-do-the-pros-outweigh-the-cons.aspx

Wu, K. J. (2021a, December 7). *Why are we still isolating vaccinated people for 10 days?* The Atlantic. https://www.theatlantic.com/science/archive/2021/12/fully-vaccinated-covid-isolation-breakthrough-transmission/620919/

Wu, K. J. (2021b, December 17). *Fully vaccinated is about to mean something else.* The Atlantic. https://www.theatlantic.com/health/archive/2021/12/fully-vaccinated-cdc-boosters/621037/

Yearwood, L. T. (2021, December 29). *The bill for my homelessness was $54,000.* The New York Times. https://www.nytimes.com/2021/12/29/opinion/debt-homelessness.html

Yong, E. (2021, December 16). *America is not ready for Omicron*. The Atlantic. https://www.theatlantic.com/health/archive/2021/12/america-omicron-variant-surge-booster/621027/

Yoon, D. (2021, December 16). *Highly vaccinated South Korea can't slow down Covid-19.* The Wall Street Journal. https://www.wsj.com/articles/highly-vaccinated-south-korea-cant-slow-down-covid-19-11639652626

Zakaria, F. (2020). *Ten lessons for a post-pandemic world.* Simon & Schuster Audio.

Zaman, M. H. (2020). *Biography of resistance: The epic battle between people and pathogens* (1st ed.). Harper Wave.

Zhang, S. (2021, December 26). *Omicron is pushing America into soft lockdown.* The Atlantic. https://www.theatlantic.com/health/archive/2021/12/omicron-soft-lockdown/621121/

Zimmer, C. (2021, December 2). *Most Covid vaccines will work as boosters, study suggests.* The New York Times. https://www.nytimes.com/2021/12/02/health/covid-booster-shots-mix-and-match.html?auth=login-google1tap&login=google1tap

Zimmer, C., Mueller, B., & Buckley, C. (2021, November 18). *First known Covid case wasvendor at Wuhan Market, scientist claims.* The New York Times. https://www.nytimes.com/2021/11/18/health/covid-wuhan-market-lab-leak.html

About the Author

Shawn A. McCastle is a Ph.D. Management (Marketing) candidate at LIGS University and a Th.D. Pastoral Theology candidate at Andersonville Theological Seminary.

McCastle completed his Ph.D. B.A. (management and organization) coursework at Trident University International. He holds an M.B.A. from the University of the People, an M.S. in industrial-organizational psychology from the School of Advanced Studies at the University of Phoenix, dual undergraduate degrees, summa cum laude, in organizational management (B.A.) and psychology (B.A.) from the University of Arizona Global Campus, and an Associate of General Studies from the Northwestern State University of Louisiana.

McCastle has worked in management and supervisory roles, including culturally sensitive positions, most of his adult life.

McCastle's doctoral research focuses on loss and grief in the workplace. His business and I-O psychology focus are on reducing AI-human conflict and executive coaching in the workplace.

To learn more about Shawn A. McCastle, visit www.shawnmccastle.com.
Twitter: @shawnmccastle
Author's Website: www.shawnmccastle.com
LinkedIn: https://www.linkedin.com/in/smccastle/

www.ingramcontent.com/pod-product-compliance
Lightning Source LLC
Chambersburg PA
CBHW060844280326
41934CB00007B/917